CW00428773

# THE 20/20 DIET COOKBOOK

## TRANSFORM YOUR LIFE AND BODY WITH HIGH-ENERGY WHOLEFOODS

TO CHARLIE GOLDSMITH: FOR BELIEVING
IN ME WHEN IT FELT LIKE NO ONE ELSE DID,
INCLUDING MYSELF. YOU'RE A LIFE CHANGER,
KEEP DOING WHAT YOU DO. THANK YOU.
LOVE, YOUR NUMBER ONE POTATO.

# THE 20/20 DIET
# COOKBOOK

## TRANSFORM YOUR LIFE AND BODY WITH HIGH-ENERGY WHOLEFOODS

# LOLA BERRY

### AUSTRALIA'S FAVOURITE NUTRITIONIST

plum    Pan Macmillan Australia

# CONTENTS

# INTRODUCTION

**When I wrote *The 20/20 Diet*, I had no idea it was going
to inspire so many people to kick-start a healthy-eating
lifestyle. I shared my story about losing 20 kilos in 20 weeks
and, as a nutritionist, I was able to explain why our bodies
hold weight and how we can take action to prevent weight
gain, promote weight loss and keep our bodies in balance.
*The 20/20 Diet* also had a few recipes to get people started,
but I was completely blown away by the number of people
who contacted me and told me how much they loved the
recipes and that they wanted *lots more*, especially ones for
veggos and vegans and people with lactose intolerance,
coeliac disease, fructose malabsorption and food allergies.
So that's why I've written *The 20/20 Diet Cookbook* — to give
you loads of new recipe ideas for using wholefoods that are
super high in nutrients and super low in allergens, with no
table sugar, no wheat, no gluten and very little dairy.**

There's something for everyone in here. It doesn't matter what
your dietary needs are, you will be able to find recipes that tick
all of your boxes. Plus I've given you plenty of suggestions to
help you tweak ingredients to suit your taste.

My goal as a nutritionist is to inspire people to be the
best version of themselves that they can be. And if this book
becomes a tool for you to become healthier and to help you to
feel your best then I will be over the moon!

My experience is both professional and also very personal.
I've battled weight problems on both sides of the spectrum.
I've been overweight and I've also been extremely underweight
— to the point where I was seriously damaging my health.
The 20/20 Diet enabled me to find the perfect balance and
to nourish every element of my being: physically, mentally,
emotionally and spiritually. This is the best I've ever felt and
I am keen to spread the message to as many people as I can!

Now, I'm not going to lie to you. Cooking my 20/20 recipes
takes a bit of effort at first. If you're not already into clean
wholefoods, you're going to have to give your pantry a bit of a
makeover. But eating clean doesn't mean living off 'rabbit food';
it's about real foods that are as close to their natural state as
possible — the stuff your body thrives on: veggies, nuts, seeds,
fruits, fish, organic meats and eggs. But forget the packet stuff

— that's no good for anyone. If you pick up a packet or tin and reading the label feels like you're in chemistry class, then put it down. Think real foods and you're set.

The best place to buy real food is at your local farmers market, because you're not only getting your hands on the freshest seasonal produce, but also supporting your local economy *and* helping to reduce your carbon footprint. Of course, not everyone can get to a farmers market, so don't feel guilty if you can't. Your local greengrocer will probably source local produce anyway, and most supermarkets are now labelling produce so you know where it's come from, as well as offering plenty of organic options and cage-free animal products. (Buying organic, ethical food means you get to vote with your dollar, and every one does make a difference.)

Cooking my 20/20 recipes also means you need to be willing to step outside your comfort zone. You may not have heard of quinoa, chia seeds or stevia or made veggie chips or cooked with coconut oil. But that's all part of the fun! I'm like a nutty professor in the kitchen — that's how I've come up with some of my most awesome creations.

In the following chapters, I will give you some tips on organising your pantry and fridge, and then we'll get straight into the recipes.

I'll give you the tools, so all you need is the sheer determination to achieve whatever your health goal may be. It might simply be to quit sugar, or to lose five kilos, or to stop drinking caffeine. Whatever it is, I'm here to tell you that you *can* do it, and that even if you do fall off the wagon (and you probably will), the real success is getting up the next day and jumping back on. I know you can do this, *you* know you can do this, otherwise you wouldn't have read this much of the book. So now's the time; start now, this second, all it takes is a decision. *You* get to choose.

The way I see it, life is too short to not soak up every second of it with every cell of your being. Realise that you deserve this. You deserve to feel great, to look great, to have an amazing life, to be happy. Use the tools in this book to make it happen. *You* have the power.

I have this theory that when you don't believe in yourself, but someone else does, it's like they give you a new set of wings. So I want you to know that I believe in you, I really do. I know you can achieve anything you want, so let's do this. It's time to fly!

WHAT TIME
IS IT? NOW.
WHERE ARE
YOU? HERE.
WHO ARE YOU?
THIS MOMENT.

## MINDFULNESS AND NOURISHMENT

I'm a nutritionist, so I know the science behind digestion,
metabolism and how nutrients (or the lack thereof) influence
every function in our brains and bodies. But as you've
probably already guessed, I'm also a bit of a hippy, and for
me, mindfulness is the key to nourishment. By mindfulness
I don't mean a 20-minute meditation session (though that
could be part of it). It's about being open, flexible and curious.
It's about paying attention to what you're doing and soaking
up every moment rather than letting your mind race ahead,
worrying about the next thing you're going to do. So when
you're shopping for your ingredients, pick the ones that feel
right and that you really want to cook with; smell them and
touch them. When you're preparing food, notice its texture and
colour, inhale its aromas, use knives and implements slowly and
gently (a hard one for me, but it works, trust me!). Turn your
mind right down. I love to listen to quirky folk stuff or even
classical music when I cook. Put loving energy into your food,
whether you are making it for yourself or for dear friends. Food
is here to nourish and fuel our bodies but also to share with the
souls we love. And when you're eating it, chew it slowly and for
longer than you normally would. Try to pick out the flavours.
Put your fork down often. You'll find you feel full much quicker.
Then enjoy cleaning up. It's all part of the process.

# WHAT IS THE 20/20 DIET?

The 20/20 Diet works by loading your body up with nutrient-dense foods and avoiding the dairy, grains and refined sugar that are common allergens. Basically, it's about eating what humans were designed to eat: unprocessed, nutritious, natural, seasonal, whole and delicious foods. Most of my clients feel better within four days (some in just 48 hours!) after cutting out the refined, sugary junk, but lives really start to change in two weeks, and I mean *really* change. That's when the magic happens, and looking good is just one part of the transformation: your skin glows, your eyes sparkle, you sleep better, your concentration improves and your whole outlook on life shifts.

## THE 20/20 DIET IN AN (ORGANIC) NUTSHELL

Eating foods that are unprocessed, seasonal, nutrient-dense, whole, natural, organic and low-GI.

You might see some similarities between this diet and a primal or paleo way of eating. This is where people eat only the kinds of wholefoods that our ancestors hunted and gathered for millennia — seeds, nuts, fruit (especially berries), vegetables, fish, shellfish, poultry and game — and shun all the foods that developed after humans settled down and began farming and processing grains and dairy foods. But I eat lots of non-paleo foods too, such as oats, quinoa and butter. For me, it's about being healthy and feeling good about what I eat, and my 20/20 Diet works for me. I hope you will do the same with the ingredients in my recipes, too. So if you really love wholefoods like rice, beans, organic soy products or goat's cheese, and your body can tolerate them then go for it! We are all different and respond in different ways to different foods. Take as much as you want from this book, try things out — your body will tell you pretty quickly if it can handle it. If you feel tired, foggy, grumpy or bloated after a meal, then steer clear of the food you think might be the culprit for a little while then reintroduce it and see how you go. This rule applies to all foods, not just grains, legumes and dairy food; some people react to fruits and even certain vegetables (such as onions or tomatoes) so it all comes back to this: listen to your body. It is your temple, honour it.

# ESSENTIAL INGREDIENTS

The key to healthy eating is being organised in the kitchen, and that means having the right ingredients to hand. Now this is going to sound obvious, but you absolutely *must* have fresh fruit, veggies and herbs in your fridge and pantry. That way, there will always be something nourishing for you to snack on or to create.

As you'll see from my recipes, raw nuts and seeds play a big part in the 20/20 Diet. They're high in protein, the good fats, vitamins and minerals, and not only add loads of flavour and texture to your meals, but also make an awesome on-the-go snack. I generally use them raw because roasting them at high temperatures affects the nutrients. I also try to soak them overnight to make them more digestible, but if I forget, I just soak them for 20 minutes. I store my nuts and seeds in jars to keep them super fresh (they look so cute all lined up!). Some of my favourite nuts and seeds are listed below, along with the other ingredients I always have in my pantry or fridge. If they're not available from your supermarket then try your local health food shop.

## ALMOND BUTTER

This is simply ground almond paste in a jar, with all its lovely oils, and is a wonderful butter substitute. I prefer mine raw (not roasted) because, you guessed it, it's the healthier option! Almonds are little powerhouses when it comes to nutritional benefits: they're loaded with fibre, good fats, protein, plus they contain a fair bit of magnesium and calcium.

## ALMOND MEAL

This healthy, grain-free flour alternative is another staple in my kitchen. (I find coconut flour a little bit heavy on my tummy, so almond meal works magic!) You can buy almond meal whole or blanched. I love the whole almond meal because it's got a coarse texture and is great in brekkie creations, for crumbing meats and fish and even in desserts and raw treats. Blanched almond meal (often called almond flour) is more refined, as the almond skin is removed before grinding.

## ALMOND MILK

Unsweetened almond milk in the pantry is very handy. It tastes delicious and you can add it to pretty much any recipe that calls for milk. I use this in most of my brekkies. You can make your own if you have an amazing food processor. (If you do make your own, don't throw away the nutty, fibrous bits; save them and use them to make energy balls or some other raw treat.)

## AVOCADOS

A quick flick through my recipes will tell you that I'm pretty keen on avocados. They're a staple in my smoothies and awesome in salads. Avos are a good source of fibre, potassium and vitamin C, and although they are high in fat, it's the good kind (unsaturated, like olive oil). My favourite variety is Hass, which has a dark, rough skin and is available all year round. (When I lived in Queensland, the farmer I bought my Hass avos from called them 'crocodile pears', after their bumpy skin!) Try to buy organic when you can — I know it costs more, but when you're making a special meal, it's worth spending a few extra dollars for the unbeatable taste and texture of organic avos.

## BEE POLLEN

Bee pollen is the soft yellow 'dust' from flowers that bees brush into the pollen sacs on their back legs. It's high in protein and nutrients and the bees use it to feed their larvae and to make royal jelly. (This is different from the nectar that they collect in their special tummy compartments, which is used to make honey.) Obviously, people with pollen allergies should steer well clear of bee pollen. Vegans might also prefer not to have it on their eating list. But it's got heaps of nutrients. I use it as a 'sprinkler' on top of pretty much any brekkie from pancakes to muesli or even porridge and it makes a delish smoothie topper — it not only looks great but also adds awesome crunch and honey pops of flavour.

## BLACK PEPPERCORNS

These are a true staple in my kitchen. I reckon freshly ground black pepper tastes loads better than the pre-ground stuff. If a recipe calls for a more subtle taste of black pepper, I just grind it up a bit more in my mortar and pestle.

## BLACK BEANS

If you can tolerate legumes, these are terrific. Also called black turtle beans, these guys are related to kidney beans and haricot (navy) beans and are widely used in American, Creole, Cajun and South American dishes. Like most legumes, they are high in protein and fibre, so a great veggie option. But don't mix them up with the black beans (douchi) used in Asian cuisines, which are actually fermented and salted soy beans. (I don't use soy products in my recipes because my body can't tolerate them. Also, I'm not keen on soy because it's a genetically modified crop.)

## BUCKWHEAT

Despite its name, buckwheat is not a grain. It's not a grass at all, but the fruit of a plant related to sorrel and rhubarb. It's sold as groats or flour. Groats are the light-coloured kernels that you can buy whole or ground (cracked) and either raw or roasted (called kasha). Buckwheat flour is available in light and dark versions. The darker type contains more of the hull, therefore more fibre and nutrients, and has a stronger, nuttier flavour. I love to use buckwheat groats for porridge or as a replacement for burghul (cracked wheat) in tabouli. Buckwheat flour makes delicious pancakes and slices and I often add it to my gluten-free creations.

## CACAO

Ah, chocolate! Technically, cacao and cocoa are the same thing, but in everyday use, cacao usually refers to the raw, unprocessed beans, and cocoa to the beans that are roasted and processed (and usually combined with stacks of milk and sugar to make chocolate).

Cacao powder is the healthiest way to get a chocolate hit: add it to a smoothie or use it to make a hot chocolate, some energy balls or a raw choccy cake. It's not only delicious, but also full of health benefits, especially for our brains. Cacao has stacks of magnesium (great for our muscles and heart) and phenylalanine, a precursor to two brain chemicals that make us feel good (norepinephrine and dopamine) — maybe that's why we love chocolate so much!

And here's a health nerd fact for you: the botanical name for the cocoa tree is *Theobroma cacao*. Theobroma means 'food of the gods', so if it's good enough for the gods then it's good enough for me!

## CHIA SEEDS

These guys provide an amazing hit of nutrients, especially protein, calcium and omega-3 fatty acids. To get the full benefits of these tiny seeds, just soak them for a bit — even five minutes is enough. They're quite gelatinous, so people use them to thicken sauces and as substitutes for eggs. (They actually swell to 17 times their original size if they're in enough liquid.) These days everyone knows how good they are so you can get them at most supermarkets. I add them to my brekkie every day, and also sprinkle them on smoothies and salads. Yep, they somehow make it into nearly every meal! Just don't boil or bake them at high temperatures as it messes with their nutrients.

## CHILLI

As you probably know, I'm completely addicted to chillies! They speed up your metabolic rate (good for weight control), promote heart health, and are full of antioxidants (fantastic for your skin). I slice them up fresh to have in salads or veggie dishes or to season meat and sometimes I even add a tiny pinch of flakes to smoothies, slices and cakes. The mildest chilli is the longish, thin cayenne chilli (it comes in red, green and yellow), followed by the medium–hot ball chilli, the hot jalapeño, the very hot tiny bird's eye chilli and the scorching habañero. I often use bird's eye chillies at home, but have used the milder cayenne chillies for most of the recipes in this book.

## COCONUT MILK AND COCONUT CREAM

These coconut products are perfect for curries, pancake mixes, porridges and even smoothies. If you use some coconut milk in your brekkie you'll be full all day! Some people confuse coconut milk and cream, but they're actually made the same way, just using different amounts of water. Coconut milk is made by simmering equal amounts of water and coconut meat and straining the mixture. Coconut cream is made the same way, but uses 1 part water to 4 parts coconut, so it is much creamier. You can make it yourself if you have the time, but I just buy mine in tins. I try to buy organic coconut cream packed in BPA-free tins. (BPA, or bisphenol-A, is a toxic chemical that works like oestrogen and can really mess with your hormones.) But if you can't get your hands on the organic stuff don't panic — the regular stuff will be perfectly fine.

## COCONUT NECTAR

Sometimes known as coconut syrup, this has a slightly stronger flavour than honey or even agave — almost like a mild molasses. It's loaded with minerals and is a great option when it comes to natural sweeteners. It contains less fructose than agave and honey, too. But remember, it's a sweetener, so use it in moderation.

## COCONUT OIL

If you haven't seen this magical stuff before, don't be surprised that it's solid at cooler temperatures. (Because I live in Melbourne mine only becomes liquid in the summer months.) Unlike olive oil, coconut oil has a high smoke point (103°C) so doesn't go rancid when we cook with it.

Now, everyone freaks out about coconut oil making them fat. Yes, coconut oil is a saturated fat, but it's a medium-chain fatty acid, which means the body can use it quickly (rather than having to store it), so it gets the green light from me. It's awesome used topically, too — I use it on my face and even do hair treatments with it. It's also thermogenic, meaning it helps to speed up your metabolism which is a bonus if you want to shed some weight. I tell my clients to pop a teaspoonful into their morning smoothies or teas. I love the stuff; I eat it straight off the spoon!

## COCONUT WATER

Coconut water is actually the fluid from inside a young coconut — a bit like Mother Nature's very own electrolyte drink. It's naturally sweet and I just love having it after a run, some weights training or a hot yoga session. It also makes a fantastic base for smoothies and if you're a bit of a cocktail fan then it's great mixed with your favourite alcohol. And the bonus is that all those electrolytes will help to prevent a hangover.

## DRIED COCONUT

I use this pretty much every day. You can get desiccated, that's the super fine stuff; then there's shredded, which are long, thin pieces; and then flaked, which is my favourite because it's chunky and chewy.

## EGGS

With eggs I always go for organic, not only because they taste unreal, but also because the chickens have access to pasture and sunlight and get to live a much better life than caged hens.

## GOJI BERRIES

These berries are an excellent source of antioxidants and have a nice flavour — not too sweet, a bit like a sourish sultana. Goji berries are fun to add to any dish (sweet or savoury) and you can sprinkle them on your brekkie, your salads, in a raw nut mix, or even in your tea. (That's my dad's new addiction; he won't have a cup of tea without his goji berries in it!)

## HERBS AND SPICES

Fresh herbs and spices are the *key* to adding flavour to your food, not to mention the antioxidant hit you'll reap from them. Some of my favourites are cinnamon, nutmeg, paprika, red chilli, chilli flakes, cumin, coriander seeds, cardamom, fennel, dill, rosemary ... the list goes on!

## LINSEED (FLAX SEED)

Linseed (also called flax seed) is a great source of fibre (it acts a bit like an intestinal broom), but is also high in omega-3 fatty acids and minerals. I always tell my vegan clients to up the flaxseeds and flaxseed oil. You can get brown flax and golden flax, but both contain the same nutrients. The gold looks super sweet in salads and even on a raw treat base, but to really release the nutrients, they need to be ground up, so I use the brown flax seeds in my breakfasts and smoothies. But I never bake or cook with it as heat destroys its nutrients.

## LSA

LSA stands for (ground) linseed, sunflower and almond, and is an awesome superfood. It's high in fibre, good fats and veggo protein, plus it has a nice hit of B vitamins. I use it in smoothies, raw creations, breakfast combos, and on top of salads. Don't cook or bake with LSA as the flax and sunflower seeds lose their nutritional benefits when heated.

## MACADAMIA NUTS AND OIL

Macadamia nuts are an excellent source of monounsaturated fats and an unreal brain food. We are so lucky to have heaps of them here in Australia; in fact, they're sometimes called 'Aussie nuts' by people overseas. I love their texture and flavour and use them in brekkies, smoothies, salads and baking. Macadamia oil is so pure I even use it on my skin! (When I was living in Queensland, my boyfriend and I would drive past macadamia plantations every weekend on our way to Byron Bay. At that time I'd decided I was going to be the Steve Irwin of fruit and veggies and I'd get him to pull over and film me while I talked excitedly to camera about the health benefits of these little gems. Poor Kane! He just wanted to get to Byron Bay for a surf. Ha ha! Thank you, Kane, for being so patient and for being such an awesome cameraman.)

## MAPLE SYRUP

I love the way maple syrup glistens when you pour it over a fresh slice of Pumpkin and Pecan Pie (see page 183)! It's an awesome sweetener: the flavour is out of this world, it's full of minerals and it contains less fructose than honey, dates or agave. Make sure you go for the real deal (the 100 per cent syrup), not the imitation stuff. Pure maple syrup costs a lot more, but is a much healthier option.

## MEDJOOL DATES

Who doesn't love a date? I've just walked into a pun, haven't I? No seriously, dates are not only lovely and sweet, but they are a great source of the electrolyte potassium which is a key player when it comes to heart health. Plus, these guys are full of fibre and will keep you super regular. I love medjool dates, which are bigger, sweeter and squidgier than regular dried dates. They taste amazing by themselves but are very sweet, so to avoid a sugar rush I pop the seed out of the middle and replace it with a Brazil nut. The protein and fat from the nut helps to lower the glycaemic load and make for a slower release of energy. You'll find medjool dates in the fridge section of the supermarket. These dates are little bits of heaven. Enjoy!

## OATS

Pure oats don't contain gluten, but because of the way we process them, most oatmeal brands have been cross-contaminated with miniscule amounts of wheat, barley and/or rye, so we can't call them 'gluten-free'. About 30 per cent of people who have coeliac disease cannot tolerate oats (even when the cross-contamination is almost eliminated), so if you have coeliac disease, or a particularly severe gluten allergy, proceed with caution, and listen to your body. I know I can't handle gluten, but I feel totally fine when I eat oats.

## OLIVE OIL, EXTRA-VIRGIN

I love olive oil not only because it imparts an unreal flavour but because it's a great source of monounsaturated fats. Olive oil has a low smoke point (43°C), so becomes unstable and rancid when used in cooking. The trick with olive oil is to use it as a dressing, or to drizzle it over cooked food. (I've even done hair treatments with olive oil, and I know mums use it for bubbas with nappy rash!) Just make sure it is extra-virgin, which means it's been pressed once, with no chemicals or additives.

## PINK SALT

Pink salt tastes just like normal salt but has loads more minerals (about 84 trace minerals in fact!). It's great to use in place of regular table salt and looks really pretty. I use Murray River or Himalayan. Celtic sea salt and rock salt are healthy options, too. Just stay away from the bleached stuff.

## POMEGRANATES

You can tell by the brilliant red colour of this fruit that it's good for you — it's packed with antioxidants. I have it fresh in my salads. To get the seeds out, you simply cut the pomegranate in half and tap the back of it with the side of a heavy knife. You can also get dried pomegranate seeds, which are delicious in salads, as well as in trail mixes and as smoothie toppers. The juice is great, but only get the 100 per cent pure juice (you'll know it's the right one because it'll be a bit tart).

## PUMPKIN SEEDS

Also called pepitas, these guys are full of zinc, which is kind of like the traffic controller of the entire body. Zinc is found in every cell of our bodies and plays a big role in immunity, cell division, cell growth, wound healing, and the breakdown of carbs. I love adding pumpkin seeds to a seed mix spiced with paprika and chilli flakes. They're yummy on top of pretty much anything.

## QUINOA

Quinoa is pronounced 'keen-wa' — weird, I know! I think of this little gem as an Aztec seed, as it is so packed with nutrients. It is very high in protein, so is a good one to include in your diet if you're a veggo or vegan. It's also versatile: you can get quinoa seeds, quinoa flakes, puffed quinoa, and even quinoa milk and quinoa flour. And there are also different types of seeds: white quinoa, red and a royal black, though they're pretty much on a par nutrient-wise (the coloured ones may have a slightly higher mineral content). I find the white has the mildest flavour, while the other two have a nuttier taste. So if you've never had it before start with the white; you cook it in a similar way to rice and it suits both sweet and savoury creations. You can use the flakes to make a sweet porridge for brekkie, the seeds as the base of a super-food salad for lunch, or served with curry for dinner, and the flour for making cakes, muffins or even pancakes. This is pretty awesome stuff!

## RAW HONEY

Raw honey has been filtered, but in a way that doesn't destroy its nutrients. It is not pasteurised (the heating and filtration process that makes it clear) so all its beneficial enzymes are still present. Raw honey can be solid at room temperature (depending on how cold it is), and is milky (not clear). It's about twice as sweet as sugar, so you don't need to use as much. I even use it in some of my face masks. Did you know that the word 'honeymoon' came about because couples drank a fermented honey drink on the night of their wedding as a libido enhancer? You do now!

## STEVIA

This sweetener is made from the leaves of a South American herb and it's about 300 times sweeter than sugar yet has no calories and no impact on blood-sugar levels. You can buy it in powder form or as a liquid (I use the liquid). However, you have to be really careful to use it sparingly. If you use more than a couple of drops you'll get hit with a pretty nasty aftertaste. It doesn't taste quite the same as sugar, but once you're used to it, you'll be converted. I use it every day!

## TAHINI

Tahini is a paste made from crushed sesame seeds. There are two types: hulled (where the seed casing has been removed) and unhulled, which is made from the whole seed. Both are high in protein and good fats. Hulled tahini is lighter in colour and has a milder taste, but unhulled has more calcium and fibre, so I tend to switch between the two. You can also get black tahini, which looks amazing and tastes similar to the hulled tahini (sesame seeds come in a variety of colours, including gold, brown, red and grey). Tahini is great in salad dressings, dips and energy ball creations.

## VANILLA PODS

Vanilla beans, like honey and cinnamon, are a great libido enhancer. These guys will dry out if left in the open air, so wrap them in foil, seal them in a zip-lock bag, and store them in a cool, dark place. Vanilla beans can be pricey, so if you prefer, you can use powdered vanilla. Make sure the powdered stuff is 100 per cent vanilla. (Watch out for imitations; the label should say 'vanilla' and nothing else.)

## YOGHURT

I'm not a big fan of cow's milk products because they don't agree with my tummy, but I do know that some people who react to cow's milk can tolerate yoghurt as it's partially fermented and is a little easier to digest. When you're buying yoghurt go for organic or biodynamic and full-cream options as there are loads more goodies in the whole versions compared to low-fat options. If you can't handle cow's milk yoghurt, try sheep's or goat's yoghurt; they have a slightly stronger flavour. Then there's coconut yoghurt for a totally vegan option.

Whatever yoghurt you choose, read the label carefully: you don't want any sugar or gelatin. We're after real foods that are as close to their natural state as possible.

## YOUR SMILE

Make your kitchen a happy place. If you feel optimistic and focused, that positive energy flows into the food you prepare. So be mindful, present and enjoy the whole process when it comes to creating, eating and sharing food. Put your heart into it and it will taste better, and nourish not only your body but your whole being. And listen to music you love while you cook; it makes the world of difference!

# HANDY EQUIPMENT

I know this sounds naff, but a clean, uncluttered kitchen is central to food preparation. Knowing where everything is and not having to clear away a messy bench before every step in your recipe saves you loads of time and, believe it or not, makes for yummier food — nothing tastes good when it's prepared by a stressed-out cook!

There are a few gadgets that are gold in my kitchen. They make food preparation a breeze and if you can possibly get these, it will be well worth your while.

## BLENDER

I'm a bit of a smoothie queen and sometimes I put nuts and dried seaweed into my combos, which can be a little tricky for a hand mixer or a standard blender, so I use a Vitamix. This makes my smoothies super silky. Get the best blender you can afford, because the end result in terms of texture, flavour and consistency is so worth it!

## FOOD PROCESSOR

Get the most powerful processor you can afford. Because I love making raw energy balls and other raw creations, I use mine all the time. This and my blender get the most use in my kitchen. I also have a little hand-held stick blender which is perfect for blending soups.

## JUICER

If you're going to get serious about juices, then it will be worth forking out for a good one. I would recommend a slow 'masticating' juicer, which retains the fibres of your fruits and veggies as opposed to spinning the fruit at high speed and just squeezing out the juice. Good brands are the Champion and the Oscar, or the Juicepresso, which is a bit cheaper.

## SLOW COOKER

I love slow cooking because it not only makes meat taste deelishimo, but it doesn't destroy all the nutrients in your food (many vitamins and amino acids are destroyed when heated at high temperatures). It's great for curries, stews, broths — you name it!

## SPIRAL VEGGIE SLICER

This gadget is brilliant because it grates your veggies in long strips so that they look just like spaghetti. It works really well on zucchinis, cucumbers and carrots, and is a great way to prepare veggies when you're sick of diced, sliced and julienned. In the raw foodie world this is a must!

## MANDOLIN SLICER

This is what I use most days, as it can slice veggies wafer-thin as well as grate and julienne. Just make sure you used the hand guard or you might accidently slice your finger (been there, done that). It's also small (it doesn't take up half your kitchen bench) and light (I've travelled with mine), and can pretty much slice anything. It can do beautiful julienned veggies, but they won't be as long as the super-long spirals of the spiral veggie slicer.

## SALAD SPINNER

A salad spinner is great for getting rid of excess moisture after you've washed lettuce or other greens, and I use mine a lot. It stops your salad from going soggy, and ensures you can taste every drop of dressing.

## DEHYDRATOR

This gadget dries fruit and veggies at a very low temperature (less than 37°C) in order to retain their nutritional value so they're still considered 'raw'. You can make yummy sweet potato crackers, kale chips, flaxseed or chia seed crackers and unbelievably delicious chilli mushroom chips. I've made dried fruit snacks of every kind from mango and strawb slices to banana discs with a squeeze of lime juice over the top. This is also how I make my activated nuts and kale chips. However, a dehydrator can set you back a bit, so if money is an issue, you can get similar results by cooking things in your oven at a really, really low heat. Grab yourself a thermometer if you're doing that at home, so you can keep an eye on the temperatures — you might even need to keep the oven door ajar to keep the temp down.

## CHEF'S KNIFE

I use my good knives every single day. If you get just one knife, make it a chef's knife — it's great for chopping everything from a slab of beef to a cherry tomato. And the better the knife the longer it will last and the easier it will be to use. Don't forget to sharpen your knife. You can do this yourself (ask for sharpening tips when you buy your knife), or pay a professional sharpener to do it (ask at a hardware store). Just one word of warning: kitchen knives can get a little addictive. I've started collecting knives and once you use a good one, there's no going back!

## CHOPPING BOARDS

Wooden chopping boards are my favourite because they feel so solid, and their rustic look adds character to my kitchen. They're pretty easy to clean, but you must make sure you have separate chopping boards for different types of foods: at least one for meat and one for veggies. I probably go a bit overboard having one each for red meat, poultry, fish, veggies and fruit and one for all of the onion family, but trust me: when you cut up a juicy mango and it has the tang of garlic you'll never use the same chopping board for everything again!

## POTS AND PANS

A good-quality frying pan with a thick base is a good idea — the thicker the base, the easier it is to control your cooking temperature. Keep away from the non-stick ones with their dodgy coatings and go for a stainless steel one. If you give it a super powerful scrub with a stainless steel scourer after the first use, nothing will stick to it again. Also consider a good stock pot with a thick base for making soups and for slow-cooking (especially if you don't want to invest in an electric slow-cooker). As you'll soon see from my recipes, I love to make grain-free slices, cakes, muffins and cupcakes, so a brownie or slice tin and a couple of 12-cup patty pans or muffin trays are essential in my kitchen. Finally, a very good-quality roasting pan is a must. A stainless steel one with a lid will set you back a bit, but will more than halve your roasting time, and you get to crisp the veggies in the lid!

## TRUSTY IMPLEMENTS

I couldn't imagine life without my wooden spoon, masher, rubber spatula, zester, whisk, mini-whisk and (wait for it) oyster shucker. Except for the shucker, I use most of these every single day — especially the mini-whisks for salad dressings. (I just had to include the shucker because I am so proud that my mates Alice and Nick taught me how to use this!)

If you get just one knife, make it a chef's knife... once you use a good one, there's no going back!

# COOKING NOTES

**Here are some notes about food preparation that I haven't included in every recipe (to avoid boring you to death).**

- Assume that any fresh fruits (bananas, mangoes, avocados etc.) are ripe, unless I say 'super ripe', in which case they need to be really ripe to make the consistency just right.

- Assume that all fresh fruits (except berries) and vegetables are washed, trimmed, cored, pitted or peeled (unless I explain that you should leave the skin on, or that you can also use the core, stalks etc.).

- I've supplied cooking temperatures for a regular or conventional ('radiant') oven, which is where you have an element or gas burner at the bottom. If you are using a fan-forced oven (which is much more efficient) you'll need to drop your cooking temperature by 10–20°C. (Check your oven manual.)

**The following ingredients appear in lots of my recipes, and I want to share a couple of tips here just in case you're not familiar with their preparation.**

- Coconut oil is solid at room temperature, so can be tricky to measure. I pop the jar into a pot of hot water to melt it.

- When I say 'nuts, soaked and rinsed' this means you pop the nuts in a bowl, cover with water and leave to soak for a good 2–3 hours (sometimes longer). This removes enzyme inhibitors and makes them easier for the body to break down and digest. If you forget to soak your nuts it's not the end of the world — even 20 minutes while you're starting to prepare a meal will have a positive effect.

- When I mention red chillies in a recipe, I'm usually referring to the long, thin cayenne chillies that you can get at any supermarket. These are quite mild compared to other varieties, but they are still very spicy. You simply trim the stem and slice them thinly, using the seeds and all. (Make sure you wash your hands after chopping them, and don't get the juice in your eyes.) If you're not big on chillies, use less than I suggest, or if you love them, by all means add more, or use the hotter varieties. I'm a big fan of bird's eye chillies (which are very hot!).

- Olive oil is always extra-virgin; this means it's the first pressing so it's going to be super fresh. Go for cold-pressed, too, if you can. This means it hasn't been exposed to heat in the pressing process. Olive oil is a monounsaturated fat so becomes unstable and rancid at around 43°C. I never cook with it, but use it for dressings or simple drizzle it over something that's already been cooked.

Soaking nuts removes enzyme inhibitors and makes them easier for the body to break down and digest.

- When I talk about seasoning with salt in my recipes, I'm not referring to table salt (which is highly processed), but to pink salt, Celtic sea salt or rock salt. But whichever you choose, please use it sparingly. It's still sodium chloride, and there's loads of research to show that excessive salt intake is linked to high blood pressure and other vascular problems.

- Quinoa (seed) needs to be rinsed before use to get rid of any residual saponins — the seed's natural protection against insects. (Quinoa imported from North America is usually cleaned, but it won't hurt to rinse it anyway — it will speed up the cooking process.)

- Medjool dates usually need to be pitted; if you don't happen to have any medjools, just use regular dried dates but soak them in water for 20 minutes first so they go a bit mooshie. If you're not keen on dates, feel free to replace them with any of the sweeteners below.

## EQUIVALENT SWEETENERS FOR 2 MEDJOOL DATES

| | |
|---|---|
| dried figs | 2–3 |
| maple syrup | 1 tablespoon |
| raw honey (unpasteurised) | 1 tablespoon |
| coconut nectar (derived from the sap of coconut palm flowers) | 1 tablespoon |
| stevia syrup (made from the leaves of a South American herb; 300 times sweeter than sugar with zero calories) | 1 drop |
| rice syrup (great for people with fructose malabsorption) | 1 tablespoon |
| coconut sugar (a granulated sugar made from the sap of coconut palm flowers) | 1 tablespoon |
| agave syrup (made from a South American succulent; around 90 per cent fructose) | 1 tablespoon |
| rapadura/panela (unrefined whole cane sugar made from dehydrated cane juice) | 1 tablespoon |
| yacon syrup (glucose-free and made from the roots of the yacon plant) | 1 tablespoon |
| lo han guo (liquid sweetener made from Chinese monkfruit) | 2–3 drops |

I bet you've heard 'breakfast is the most important meal of the day' a thousand times, but I'm here to tell you again — you can't skip brekkie and expect to stay lean and healthy. When you skip brekkie, your body goes into starvation mode, slowing your metabolism so that you hold onto your fat stores. And when you finally do eat something, your blood sugar is so low that you're more tempted to dive into those sugary muffins or cupcakes, which are then (you guessed it) stored as fat.

A good brekkie has a nice hit of protein such as eggs, yoghurt, nuts or seeds, as well as some slow-release carbs such as oats, quinoa or buckwheat so that you feel full for longer and are more inclined to make smarter food choices. All the recipes in this section are goodies — they'll kick-start your metabolism, setting you up for a great day. Most are gluten- and dairy-free, plus I've combined plant proteins for vegetarians and vegans. They're also sweetened with natural sweeteners such as raw honey, raisins or dates to keep your blood sugar levels nice and even. Many of these recipes are also versatile enough to use for lunches, dinners or even desserts! I've also designed them so that it is really easy for you to change ingredients to suit your taste.

Even if you do nothing else to change your diet, eat my healthy brekkies for a week and I promise you that you'll be feeling energised and inspired!

# BREKKIES

# QUINOA AND BLACKBERRY PORRIDGE

100 g (½ cup) white quinoa
250 ml (1 cup) almond milk
½ vanilla pod, split and
   scraped
130 g (1 cup) blackberries
2 tablespoons maple syrup
chia seeds, to serve

## TIPS

If you don't have blackberries, don't sweat. You can use blueberries, strawberries, raspberries or any kind of berries — fresh or frozen. (Yes, frozen berries contain the same amount of vitamins and fibre as fresh ones.) Also, you can substitute ¼ teaspoon of pure vanilla powder if you don't have a vanilla pod.

**This is my kind of everyday brekkie! Gluten-free, dairy-free and loaded with nutrients. I like to use white quinoa in this recipe as it has a soft flavour and creamy texture, but any variety of quinoa will work — they all have the same amount of protein, carbohydrate and fat.**

Rinse the quinoa in a fine-mesh sieve and transfer to a small saucepan with 1 cup of water. Bring to the boil, then cover, reduce heat and cook for 5–10 minutes, until the water is absorbed and the quinoa has softened and doubled in size. Add the almond milk, vanilla seeds and half the berries. Cook for another 5 minutes, or until nice and creamy.

Spoon the quinoa into two serving bowls and top each with half the remaining berries, maple syrup and a sprinkle of chia seeds. Yum!

SERVES 2

# COCONUT AND BANANA PANCAKES

4 bananas, roughly mashed
4 eggs, lightly beaten
750 ml (3 cups) almond milk
60 g (½ cup) coconut flour
220 g (1½ cups) buckwheat
    flour
¼ teaspoon gluten-free
    baking powder
¼ teaspoon ground cinnamon
1 vanilla pod, split and
    scraped
2 tablespoons maple syrup,
    optional
3 tablespoons coconut oil
coconut ice cream, optional
extra maple syrup, to serve
shredded coconut, to serve

## TIPS

If almond milk isn't your preference, coconut milk tastes just as good. Also, these pancakes are quite thick, so if you prefer yours thinner, just add an extra cup of liquid (almond milk, coconut milk or water). Gluten-free baking powder is available at most supermarkets (just check the label). And use ½ teaspoon of pure vanilla powder if you don't have a vanilla pod.

**This recipe uses coconut flour and buckwheat flour instead of wheat flour and the end result is not only super tasty but also *very* healthy. And if you really want to impress someone, top the pancakes with a scoop of delicious coconut ice cream. You can buy this from health food stores and it is free of dairy, gluten and sugar.**

Preheat the oven to 140°C. Place a baking tray in the oven to warm.

Meanwhile, combine the bananas, eggs and almond milk in a large bowl and mix well. Fold through the coconut flour, buckwheat flour, baking powder, cinnamon and vanilla seeds. If you want sweeter pancakes, add the maple syrup.

Heat the coconut oil in a frying pan over a medium heat and pour ¼ cup of pancake batter in the centre of the pan. If you like your pancakes thinner, tilt the pan so the mixture spreads. When you see little bubbles form in the middle of the pancake and the edges start to crisp up, it's time to flip it over. Cook for another 1–3 minutes, or until golden brown and cooked through — cooking time will depend on the pancake's thickness. Slide the pancake onto the baking tray so it stays warm while you whip up the rest.

When you're ready to serve, top pancakes with a scoop of coconut ice cream (if using), a drizzle of maple syrup and a sprinkle of shredded coconut.

SERVES 4

# SPICY CHAI PORRIDGE WITH BANANA

**I use spices in heaps of my recipes for their delicious flavour and their antioxidants. This banana porridge recipe uses a beautiful combination of chai spices, but if you don't have them all, even just cinnamon will do the trick.**

Place the almond meal and almond milk in a small saucepan. Stir over a low heat for a few minutes until slightly thickened. (It's important to keep the heat low because almonds contain the good unsaturated fats that become rancid when cooked at high temperatures.) Add 1 tablespoon of the chopped almonds, all of the spices and stir for another minute or so.

Divide the porridge between two bowls. Top each with slices of banana, the remaining almonds and a tablespoon of maple syrup drizzled over in a swirly pattern.

SERVES 2

50 g (½ cup) almond meal
250 ml (1 cup) almond milk
2 tablespoons roughly
   chopped almonds
pinch ground cinnamon
pinch ground cloves
pinch ground nutmeg
pinch ground cardamom
1 banana, sliced
2 tablespoons maple syrup

# CARROT CAKE PORRIDGE

120 g (1 cup) quinoa flakes
500 ml (2 cups) almond milk
1 carrot, grated
80 g (½ cup) raisins
4 medjool dates, pitted and
   roughly chopped
½ teaspoon ground cinnamon
¼ teaspoon ground ginger
¼ teaspoon ground nutmeg
pinch salt
50 g (½ cup) walnuts, roughly
   chopped
extra raisins, to serve
extra ground cinnamon,
   to serve

**If you love carrot cake but want to avoid sugar and fat, this healthy breakfast recipe is perfect for you. It really tastes like carrot cake, is super warming and the spices help to kick-start your metabolism.**

Place the quinoa flakes and almond milk in a saucepan over a medium heat and stir to combine. Add the carrot, dried fruit, spices and salt. Bring to the boil, then reduce heat and simmer for 10–15 minutes or until thick and porridgey. Serve topped with walnuts, raisins and cinnamon.

## SERVES 2

## TIPS

Feel free to use sultanas if you don't have raisins. Also, use 2 teaspoons of freshly grated ginger instead of the dried if you have it (it's great for digestion and circulation).

# STRAWBERRY AND ALMOND PANCAKES

3 eggs, lightly beaten
375 ml (1½ cups) almond milk
½ vanilla pod, split and
  scraped
3 drops stevia
400 g (4 cups) almond meal
2 teaspoons baking powder
350 g (2½ cups) strawberries,
  hulled and roughly chopped
3 tablespoons coconut oil
500 ml (2 cups) 100% pure
  pomegranate juice
1 tablespoon coconut nectar
sheep's yoghurt, to serve,
  optional
extra strawberries, to serve
chopped almonds, to serve

**I know this recipe sounds really fancy, but pomegranate syrup only takes a few minutes to make and is so delicious and nutritious that you won't be able to resist. Of course, if you are really time-poor, then these pancakes are just as yummy with maple syrup.**

Preheat the oven to 160°C and pop a serving plate in to warm.

In a small bowl whisk together the eggs, almond milk, vanilla seeds and stevia drops. (Don't overdo it with the stevia because it's 300 times sweeter than sugar and has a really bitter aftertaste.)

Place the almond meal and baking powder in a large bowl and stir to combine. Make a well in the centre and gradually add the egg mixture, stirring slowly in little circles so the almond meal doesn't clump up. Mix until you have a nice smooth batter, then add the strawberries.

Heat some coconut oil in a frying pan over a medium heat. Pop ¼ cup of the batter into the pan (the strawbs will be little lumps of pink deliciousness). If you want a thinner pancake, tilt the pan to allow the batter to spread evenly. Cook until the edges are beginning to crisp and air bubbles form in the centre (about 3 minutes). Flip the pancake and cook the other side for 1–3 minutes (depending on its thickness). Place on your warming plate in the oven. Repeat with the remaining coconut oil and batter until all of your pancakes are warming in the oven.

Pour pomegranate juice into a small saucepan and place over a medium heat. Bring to the boil. Reduce heat, add coconut nectar and simmer, uncovered, for 15–20 minutes or until the liquid is reduced, thick and syrupy. (If it starts splattering and spitting then it's too hot — you just want it to be bubbling away.) Remove from heat.

Place 2 pancakes on a plate and serve with a dollop of sheep's yoghurt (if using), a few strawbs, a sprinkle of chopped almonds and a generous drizzle of pomegranate syrup! Yumbo!

MAKES 16–18 PANCAKES

# BUCKWHEAT PORRIDGE WITH PEAR AND FIGS

100 g (½ cup) buckwheat
  groats
350 ml (1½ cups) almond milk
2 tablespoons pumpkin seeds
3 dried figs, roughly chopped
pinch ground cinnamon
pinch ground nutmeg
1 pear, grated
2 tablespoons maple syrup,
  to serve

## TIPS

You'll need to start this recipe
the night before. And if figs
aren't your thing, use medjool
dates instead.

**Buckwheat is actually a seed not a grain, and is related to
the rhubarb family. It's a great source of protein, fibre and
the bioflavonoid rutin, which can help with blood pressure.
Roasted buckwheat is sometimes called kasha, and has
a lovely, nutty flavour. You can use either raw or roasted
groats for this recipe ('groats' is just the word for any seed
or grain that's had its outer hull removed, but is still whole).
The pumpkin seeds in this recipe up the protein, so it's a real
goodie for veggos.**

Combine the buckwheat, almond milk, 1 tablespoon of the
pumpkin seeds, the dried figs, spices and grated pear in a large
bowl. Cover and refrigerate overnight (this softens the buckwheat
and makes it easier for the body to absorb its nutrients).

In the morning, spoon the mixture into two bowls and top with
maple syrup and the remaining pumpkin seeds. Job done!

SERVES 2

# QUINOA AND DATE PORRIDGE

**This one's an all-round winner! You can use any type of quinoa: white, red, royal black or a combo (the red and royal black just take a little longer to cook and have a slightly nuttier flavour). You can also try it with any kind of nut milk. Make a big batch and take it to work for a few days. It's easily reheated, but also tastes pretty awesome cold.**

Place the quinoa in a fine-mesh sieve and rinse under cold water. Pop the quinoa and almond milk in a saucepan over a medium heat and bring to the boil. Reduce the heat, add the dates, cinnamon and salt and cook for a further 5–10 minutes. The quinoa is cooked when it is puffy and has little 'tails'. To serve, spoon into bowls, drizzle over maple syrup and top with chopped pecans.

SERVES 2

200 g (1 cup) white quinoa
500 ml (2 cups) almond milk
8 medjool dates, pitted and
  roughly chopped
½ teaspoon ground cinnamon
pinch salt
2 tablespoons maple syrup
60 g (½ cup) pecans, roughly
  chopped

# BERRY BIRCHER

100 g (1 cup) rolled oats

30 g (¼ cup) pumpkin seeds

15 g (¼ cup) shredded
  coconut

30 g (¼ cup) goji berries

35 g (¼ cup) dried
  blueberries

40 g (¼ cup) raisins

1 large Granny Smith apple,
  skin on, grated

½ teaspoon ground cinnamon

¼ teaspoon ground nutmeg

400 ml (1½ cups) almond
  milk

90 g (⅓ cup) yoghurt

2 heaped tablespoons LSA

4 fresh figs, quartered

80 ml (⅓ cup) maple syrup

extra goji berries, to serve

extra ground cinnamon and
  nutmeg, to serve

**Bircher muesli is my dad's all-time favourite breakfast, so I had to put this in. Bircher is perfect if you're time-poor because you can make a big batch that will last a few days stored in the fridge and all you need to do is change your toppings: fresh banana one day, frozen berries the next, passionfruit and shredded coconut or stewed rhubarb the day after — whatever you fancy!**

In a large bowl or cereal jar, combine the oats, seeds, coconut, berries and raisins and mix well. Mix in the grated apple, spices and almond milk. Cover (or seal jar) and refrigerate overnight.

In the morning, take out a quarter of your muesli and serve with a heaped tablespoon of yoghurt, ½ tablespoon of LSA, 1 fresh fig, a tablespoon of maple syrup, and a sprinkle of goji berries, cinnamon and nutmeg.

## MAKES 4 SERVES

### TIPS

If you can't tolerate oats, this recipe also works really well with quinoa flakes. Also, keep the skin on your apple for extra fibre and nutrients.

# GLUTEN-FREE GRANOLA WITH DRIED BERRIES

**I love crunchy granola (you might know this as toasted muesli) and when I first developed the 20/20 Diet I thought I would have to say goodbye to it. Thankfully, it didn't take me long to come up with this gluten- and guilt-free recipe using cracked buckwheat groats. It's also a great one to experiment with. You could try raisins or sultanas instead of the goji berries; raw honey instead of maple syrup and nuts instead of seeds. The sky's the limit!**

Preheat the oven to 180°C and line a tray with baking paper.

Place the buckwheat, quinoa, seeds, coconut and berries in a large bowl and mix well. (I love using my hands as they do a better job than any spoon, and it also feels like I'm adding a little bit of extra love to the recipe.)

In a small bowl or jug, combine the maple syrup, melted coconut oil, cinnamon, nutmeg and salt with ⅓ cup of warm water (cooled boiled water). Pour over the dry ingredients and mix thoroughly (I use a wooden spoon for this part!). Spoon the mixture into the baking tray and press evenly over the base. Bake for 30–45 minutes, or until golden brown.

Store in an airtight container or glass jar and enjoy all week long for brekkie, a snack or even dessert!

SERVES 6

170 g (1 cup) buckwheat groats
40 g (⅓ cup) quinoa flakes
50 g (⅓ cup) pumpkin seeds
40 g (⅓ cup) sunflower seeds
20 g (⅓ cup) shredded coconut
50 g (⅓ cup) dried blueberries
30 g (¼ cup) dried cranberries
30 g (¼ cup) goji berries
80 ml (⅓ cup) maple syrup
80 ml (⅓ cup) coconut oil, melted
1 teaspoon ground cinnamon
pinch ground nutmeg
pinch salt

# CHIA AND COCONUT PUDDING WITH MANGO

80 g (½ cup) chia seeds
250 ml (1 cup) coconut milk
2 tablespoons shredded
   coconut
½ vanilla pod, split and
   scraped
2 tablespoons maple syrup
1 large mango
½ lime
extra shredded coconut,
   to serve

TIP
If you don't have vanilla pods
to hand, just use a ¼ teaspoon
of pure powdered vanilla.

**This is not only quick to whip up, but also easy to tailor to suit your tastebuds. Change any of the nuts, berries, dried or fresh fruit to whatever tickles your fancy. This one needs to be prepared the night before.**

Place the chia seeds, coconut milk, shredded coconut, vanilla seeds and maple syrup in a bowl or jar and give them a good mix. Cover or seal and place in the fridge overnight.

In the morning, divide your pudding between two serving bowls. Top with freshly cut cubes of mango, a squeeze of lime juice, a sprinkle of lime zest (freshly grated) and some shredded coconut. If it's not quite sweet enough, by all means give it another drizzle of maple syrup.

SERVES 2

# OLD SCHOOL OATS WITH MACADAMIAS

**If you're like me and gluten-intolerant, but okay with oats, this brekkie is a real treat. You see, pure oatmeal doesn't actually contain gluten, but because of the way we process it, most of our oatmeal is cross-contaminated with wheat, barley and/or rye. Even when manufacturers reduce this contamination to miniscule amounts (such as 20 parts per million), one in three people with a severe allergy to gluten (coeliac disease) will still have a reaction, so listen to your body.**

Place the oats, nut milk, coconut oil and cinnamon in a saucepan over a medium heat. Bring to the boil, reduce heat and simmer for 5–7 minutes, or until oats are soft and creamy. Remove from heat and spoon into serving bowls. Top with sliced banana, chopped maca nuts, maple syrup and a dusting of ground cinnamon. The perfect warming breakfast!

SERVES 2

100 g (1 cup) rolled oats
500 ml (2 cups) nut milk
1 heaped tablespoon
   coconut oil
½ teaspoon ground cinnamon
1 banana, sliced
100 g (1 cup) macadamia
   nuts, roughly chopped
2 tablespoons maple syrup
extra ground cinnamon,
   to serve

TIP
Any nut milk is fine: almond, coconut, hazelnut or Brazil nut — whatever blows your hair back.

# PUMPKIN, ZUCCHINI AND ALMOND LOAF

**This is one of my super-versatile recipes: you can have it for breakfast as a sweet version, or you can make it a savoury lunch or snack by topping it with mashed avocado and cherry tomatoes. Either way, it's a beauty and keeps for a few days.**

Preheat the oven to 160°C. Line a loaf tin with baking paper.

Place the pumpkin, zucchini, eggs and macadamia oil in a large mixing bowl and mix well (it should look like a gluggy mess – see pic opposite!). Add the almond meal, baking powder, salt and ground nutmeg, and mix until there are no lumps of almond meal. Spoon the mixture into the loaf tin, sprinkle the top with pumpkin seeds and place in the oven.

Now this one takes a while to bake, so after 1 hour, insert a skewer in the middle to see if it's still gooey. If it doesn't come out clean, the loaf may need another 15–25 minutes.

When cooked, remove from the oven and allow to cool slightly. While still warm, cut two slices, spread them with a little tahini, top with a drizzle of raw honey and a tiny pinch of nutmeg, and eat! This meal will always put you in a good mood.

MAKES 1 LOAF

230 g (2 cups) grated
   pumpkin
135 g (1 cup) grated zucchini
4 eggs, lightly beaten
3 tablespoons macadamia oil
300 g (3 cups) almond meal
2 teaspoons baking powder
pinch salt
pinch ground nutmeg
2 tablespoons pumpkin seeds
unhulled tahini, to serve
raw honey, to serve
extra ground nutmeg,
   to serve

# GREEN EGGS

6 eggs

40 g (1 cup) baby spinach
leaves, roughly chopped

40 g (1 cup) finely chopped
kale, stalks removed

pinch chilli flakes

10 kalamata olives, pitted
and roughly chopped

salt, to taste

freshly ground black pepper,
to taste

1 tablespoon coconut oil

30 g (1 cup) rocket

1 avocado, sliced

2 tablespoons olive oil

**Eggs are one of my favourite brain foods, so this is the perfect meal if you've got a massive day ahead. I will warn you, though: this dish might look a bit like monster food, but it's healthy, really quick and tastes yummy!**

Crack the eggs into a bowl and lightly whisk. Add the spinach, kale, chilli flakes, olives, salt and pepper, and mix well.

Heat the coconut oil in a small frying pan over a medium heat. Pour half of your egg mixture into the pan and cook for about 4 minutes, or until it's firm and there are no runny bits. Using a spatula, fold one half over the other like a regular omelette. Place on a warmed plate. Repeat with the remaining egg mixture. Serve each topped with fresh rocket, avocado slices and a drizzle of olive oil.

## SERVES 2

## TIPS

If you're in a hurry, use (thawed) frozen spinach. Also, if you don't fancy kale, you can use chard (silverbeet) instead.

# SWEET POTATO AND ZUCCHINI FRITTERS

**The lime, cucumber and yoghurt dressing makes this recipe a winner! I usually use goat's or sheep's milk yoghurt as I find them much easier to digest, but feel free to use yummy Greek-style natural yoghurt if you're totally fine with dairy.**

Place the grated zucchini in a sieve and press down firmly to remove excess liquid. Transfer to a sheet of paper towel (or a clean tea towel) and give it another squeeze. (It should feel pretty dry now.)

In a large mixing bowl combine the zucchini, grated sweet spud, onion, fresh coriander and eggs. Mix well. Add the almond meal, ground coriander, cumin and seasoning. Scoop heaped tablespoonfuls of the mixture and use your hands to form them into 8 medium-sized fritters. Pop them all on a plate.

Heat the coconut oil in a large frying pan over a medium heat. Place the fritters in the pan (you may need to cook them in batches), squooshing them down slightly with the back of a spatula. Cook the fritters on each side for 3 minutes, or until golden brown. Rest them on paper towel.

Combine the yoghurt, lime juice, zest and cucumber in a small bowl and season to taste. Serve fritters with a dollop of lime dressing.

SERVES 4

2 zucchini, grated
1 sweet potato, grated
1 red onion, finely sliced
15 g (½ cup) coriander leaves, roughly chopped
3 eggs, lightly beaten
100 g (1 cup) almond meal
½ teaspoon ground coriander
½ teaspoon ground cumin
salt, to taste
freshly ground black pepper, to taste
3 tablespoons coconut oil
250 g (1 cup) plain yoghurt
juice of 1 lime
zest of ½ lime
1 cucumber, diced

### TIP

I keep the skin on my sweet spud because it contains loads of health benefits and I love the rustic look it gives to a dish. Just wash it well.

# FIELD MUSHROOMS WITH HERB BUTTER AND AVOCADO MASH

**This one is quick, easy and jam-packed with nutrients! If you can't find field mushies, portobellos are fine (portobellos are just the grown-up versions of white button mushies).**

Preheat the oven to 180°C. Clean your mushies by brushing the dirt off (don't wash them, as it makes them soggy). Arrange them on a greased baking tray with the little gill bits facing upwards. Combine the butter, garlic and thyme in a small bowl, season to taste and mix well. Place a quarter of the herb butter on each mushie. Bake in the oven for 10–15 minutes, or until tender.

Meanwhile, halve and stone your avocados and scoop out the flesh with a spoon. Place the flesh in a bowl and mash with the back of a fork. Add the olive oil and continue mashing (it helps to make it creamier). Add the onion, cherry tomatoes, lime juice and zest, chilli flakes, coriander, salt and pepper, and moosh it all together.

To serve, place two mushrooms on a plate, drizzle with a little olive oil and pop some avo mash on the side. Deelishimo!

SERVES 2

4 large field mushrooms
1 tablespoon butter
2 garlic cloves, finely chopped
4 thyme sprigs, leaves picked and finely chopped
salt
freshly ground black pepper
2 large avocados
2 tablespoons olive oil
¼ red onion, finely diced
4 cherry tomatoes, quartered
juice and zest of 1 lime
pinch chilli flakes
30 g (1 cup) coriander leaves, chopped
olive oil, to serve

## TIPS

If you're dairy-intolerant, simply use 1 tablespoon of coconut oil in place of the butter. Also, I keep the stalks on my mushies, but feel free to trim yours if you prefer.

I *love love love* smoothies! Firstly, they're little powerhouses when it comes to health benefits, and the recipes here are packed with fruit, veggies, nuts and seeds so you get all the fibre, vitamins, minerals, antioxidants and other phytonutrients you need. Secondly, they taste great (I've experimented long enough with these little beauties to ensure that you get the very best combos!). Thirdly, they're quick to make (needing only a little nut-soaking or banana-freezing overnight). And finally, they make an awesome meal any time of day — I have them for brekkie, lunch or even dinner!

You'll need a strong food processor when using nuts in smoothies. I use a Vitamix blender and I've never looked back. A general rule of thumb, the more expensive the processor, the more efficient it will be. I know they can be quite costly but it's worth the investment if you're going to get serious about your health!

When you're making smoothies, depending on the ingredients, your processing time can be anywhere from 1 to 3 minutes. Sometimes I will blend everything up, and then give it another 30 seconds at the end to make sure it's nice and creamy. As a general rule, the longer you blend it, the smoother the consistency!

You'll notice that I use frozen bananas in lots of my smoothies. That's because I love the texture and sweetness they give! Plus, they've got a bit more glucose than fructose, so people with fructose malabsorption can often tolerate small serves. On top of that they are full of potassium, a key electrolyte (electrolytes play a crucial role in hydration, blood pH, and the body's nerve and muscle function). But, please don't forget to peel your narnies before you freeze them (it's not fun to peel them afterwards!).

# SMOOTHIES AND JUICES

## MILK ALTERNATIVES

I often use coconut water and almond milk in my smoothies, but there are *heaps* of milk alternatives, such as milk made from oats, rice, cashews, macadamia nuts, quinoa and hazelnuts. It's easy to make your own if you have a really good food processor. The ratio is 1 cup of nuts to 2 cups of water. (You'll need to soak them overnight first, and give them a good rinse.) Strain through a fine mesh sieve and you're done! (You can save the fibrous bits and use them for a raw treat recipe, or simply add them to a granola mix.)

If you don't have time to make your own nut milk, you can buy it off the shelf. Just read the labels and stay away from the stuff with loads of sugars or sweeteners. And watch out for preservatives. There should be about four ingredients and you should be able to pronounce all of them. If you can't (or they are just numbers), look them up to see if they come from a natural source.

## SWEETENER OPTIONS

Sweetners are another ingredient in my smoothies that you can easily change to suit you. There's coconut nectar, maple syrup, stevia, dates, figs, agave, raw honey, rice syrup, coconut palm sugar, rapadura (also called penala) and yacon syrup — have I forgotten anything? Remember that even natural sweeteners should only be used to slightly sweeten something; they shouldn't be guzzled down just because you bought them from a health food store. I fell into that trap before I understood my body. I used to eat a whole packet of dates or used stacks of agave in my smoothies.

If you can't tolerate too much fructose then you need to be careful with sweeteners such as agave and honey. My advice? Try a little first. Some people don't like the aftertaste of stevia while I quite enjoy it. It's about trying things out and finding what works best for you. If you feel bloated, grumpy or lethargic after using a particular sweetener, try something else.

I'm a texture girl so I love things with crunch, which is why I nearly always top my smoothies with a little something nutty, seedy or dried fruity.

## SMOOTHIE TOPPERS

These smoothie topper combos are an easy way to make your smoothies more interesting. Mix up a few of these on a weekend and keep in jars ready to top your smoothies during the week. These little recipes should give you about 6 serves.

- ½ cup each of sunflower seeds, pumpkin seeds and dried cranberries
- ½ cup each of goji berries and roughly chopped walnuts
- ½ cup each of chia seeds, roughly chopped almonds and dried blueberries
- ½ cup each of shredded coconut, pumpkin seeds and white mulberries or goji berries
- ½ cup each of roughly chopped Brazil nuts, pecans and bee pollen
- ½ cup pistachios, ¼ cup shredded coconut, ½ cup dried cranberries
- ½ cup each of sunflower seeds, shredded coconut and dried pomegranate seeds or goji berries

- ½ cup each of roughly chopped walnuts and dried figs, ¼ cup rolled oats, a pinch of nutmeg and ¼ teaspoon ground cinnamon
- ½ cup cacao nibs, ¼ cup chia seeds
- ½ cup goji berries, ¼ cup shredded coconut

These are also easy-peasy toppers, but need to be made fresh so are good for one or two smoothies at a time.

- ¼ cup roughly chopped macadamia nuts mixed with zest of ½ a lemon
- 1 teaspoon chopped mint leaves and 2 tablespoons goji berries

## RASPBERRY, LIME AND COCONUTTY DELIGHT

### TIP
If you don't want to use cashews, macadamia nuts work really well.

## THE BIG GREEN ONE
SEE PAGE 60

## PECAN AND PUMPKIN PIE SPICE SMOOTHIE

### TIP
If you can't find pumpkin pie spice, simply make your own by mixing together 1 tablespoon cinnamon, 2 teaspoons ground ginger, ½ teaspoon allspice, ½ teaspoon nutmeg, ½ teaspoon ground cloves and a pinch of ground cardamom (or mace).

# RASPBERRY, LIME AND COCONUTTY DELIGHT

**This is another flavour combo that's almost too good to be true! I've even made this extra thick and had it as an after-dinner treat.**

Pop the raspberries, lime zest (reserving a little for your garnish), lime juice, cashews, coconut oil, coconut milk and coconut nectar into your blender and process for about 60 seconds. Check the consistency, and add water if you want it a bit thinner. Pour into glasses (or bowls) and top with fresh berries, shredded coconut and the reserved lime zest. It looks super pretty.

SERVES 2

270 g (2 cups) frozen
   raspberries
zest and juice of 1 lime
75 g (½ cup) cashews, soaked
   and rinsed
2 tablespoons coconut oil
500 ml (2 cups) coconut milk
2 tablespoons coconut
   nectar
fresh raspberries, to serve
shredded coconut, to serve,
   optional

# PECAN AND PUMPKIN PIE SPICE SMOOTHIE

**I *love* pumpkin pie spice! It's so warming and jam-packed with health benefits. Cinnamon helps to balance blood sugar levels and ginger stimulates the circulatory system, has an anti-inflammatory effect on the body and is great for settling an upset tummy. This is another one of those recipes that feels like you're having a dessert, but you're actually giving your body all kinds of goodness!**

Place the banana, pecans, almond butter, spice, maple syrup and almond milk in your blender and process until smooth. Pour into bowls, mugs, glasses, cups (whatever tickles your fancy), and top with a pinch of pumpkin pie spice and a scattering of chopped pecans and chia seeds.

SERVES 2

1 frozen banana
100 g (1 cup) pecans
2 tablespoons almond butter
½ teaspoon pumpkin pie spice
2 tablespoons maple syrup
500 ml (2 cups) almond milk
pinch pumpkin pie spice,
   to serve
pecans, roughly chopped, to
   serve
chia seeds, to serve

# THE BIG GREEN ONE

← PICTURED ON PAGE 58

2 frozen bananas

75 g (½ cup) cashews, soaked
   and rinsed

170 g (4 cups) baby spinach
   leaves

1 large avocado

2 tablespoons coconut oil

2 tablespoons desiccated
   coconut

6 medjool dates, pitted

½ teaspoon ground cinnamon

500 ml (2 cups) coconut
   water

## TO SERVE

30 g (¼ cup) pumpkin seeds

30 g (¼ cup) goji berries

15 g (¼ cup) shredded
   coconut

maple syrup

**When I realised I was a health nerd, green smoothies were one of the first things that became a daily ritual. I'm now certain that there are as many green smoothie combos as there are people in the world! This is my favourite combo, but feel free to tweak ingredients to suit you. I like mine in a bowl, but if you want yours in glass, add some more coconut water. This one is worthy of a hashtag (#yumbo) and putting up on all your social media pages!**

Place the frozen narnies, cashews, baby spinach, avocado, coconut oil, desiccated coconut, medjool dates, cinnamon and coconut water into the blender and whizz it all up. The longer you process it, the smoother it will be. Depending on the power of your blender, it should take 30–60 seconds to get a nice consistency. Pour into bowls, top with pumpkin seeds, goji berries and shredded coconut, and drizzle with a touch of maple syrup.

## SERVES 2

## TIPS

Don't forget to peel your bananas before you freeze them. Also, soaking cashews overnight makes them easier to digest, but no sweat if you don't soak them — they'll still taste amazing. And if you don't have any shredded coconut for the top, desiccated is totally fine. Lastly, if you're not a fan of medjool dates, substitute 2 tablespoons of raw honey, maple syrup or coconut nectar.

# KICK-STARTER

**It might sound a little bizarre to use chilli in a smoothie, but don't worry — this tastes nothing like a savoury Mexican dish! The chilli provides antioxidants, speeds up your metabolism and supports your cardiovascular system.**

Pop everything except the fresh berries into the blender. Process until super smooth, pour into glasses and top with whatever fresh berries you have to hand. If you can't find any freshies, use dried gojis or unsweetened dried cranberries.

## SERVES 2

## TIPS

If you're not a fan of medjool dates, replace them with your choice of natural sweetener, such as 2 tablespoons of maple syrup or raw honey. And don't worry if you forget to soak the cashews; it won't affect the flavour, it's just to help with nutrient absorption.

40 g (1 cup) baby spinach leaves
1 frozen banana
150 g (1 cup) blueberries, fresh or frozen
pinch cayenne pepper
½ teaspoon ground cinnamon
3 medjool dates, pitted
75 g (½ cup) cashews, soaked and rinsed
125 ml (½ cup) almond milk
75 g (½ cup) fresh berries, to serve

# AVOCADO-COCONUT DREAMBOAT
SEE PAGE 64

## TIPS

If you don't have coconut nectar, you can use the same amount of raw honey, maple syrup or rice syrup, or 3 drops of stevia if you're a fan. It's all good. Also, don't sweat if you haven't had the time to soak the cashews, it won't affect the taste or texture, it just helps you digest all their nutrients.

# BERRY BLITZ

# CRUNCHY CHOC-MINT SMOOTHIE

# CRUNCHY CHOC-MINT SMOOTHIE

**This combo is not only great for antioxidants and digestion, but will give you a totally natural energy boost. I love making it after a run first thing in the morning!**

Pop the banana, mint leaves, cashews, cacao nibs and powder, maple syrup and almond milk into the blender and process until everything is smooth except for the nibs (the idea is to keep a nice crunch). Pour into glasses and top with cacao nibs and a sprig of fresh mint.

SERVES 2

1 frozen banana
40 g (1 cup) mint leaves
75 g (½ cup) cashews, soaked and rinsed
2 tablespoons cacao nibs
25 g (¼ cup) cacao powder
2 tablespoons maple syrup
500 ml (2 cups) almond milk
extra cacao nibs, to serve
mint sprigs, to serve

# BERRY BLITZ

**Blueberries probably get more publicity than any other fruit or veggie — nearly everyone knows how nutritious they are. This recipe is probably my favourite berry recipe of all, so when blueberries aren't in season, I use frozen ones. Try this and you'll see why it hits the spot.**

Pop everything into the blender and whizz until smooth (about 40 seconds should do the trick). This one goes a lovely purple colour, so looks super impressive. (Kids go crazy for this one. My little cousins call it 'Magic Monster Goo'!)

SERVES 2

300 g (2 cups) blueberries, plus a few extra, to serve
150 g (1 cup) cashews, soaked and rinsed
2 tablespoons coconut nectar
2 tablespoons coconut oil
500 ml (2 cups) coconut water
½ vanilla pod, split and scraped

# AVOCADO-COCONUT DREAMBOAT

← PICTURED ON PAGE 62

1 avocado

1 frozen banana

2 tablespoons coconut oil

80 g (2 cups) baby spinach
   leaves

½ vanilla pod, split and
   scraped

500 ml (2 cups) coconut
   cream

2 tablespoons desiccated
   coconut

2 tablespoons coconut nectar

1 tablespoon shredded
   coconut

extra coconut nectar, to serve

75 g (½ cup) berries, to serve

**I know 'avocado smoothie' sounds weird, but trust me, it will
make your smoothies the best consistency ever, plus your body
will soak up the avo's amazing fibre, vitamins and healthy fats.**

Scoop out the avocado and place in your blender with the
banana, coconut oil, spinach, vanilla seeds, coconut cream,
desiccated coconut and coconut nectar. Process until silky
smooth. Pour into tall glasses and garnish with a sprinkle of
shredded coconut, drizzle of coconut nectar and a few berries
of your choice. It's hard to believe such a sweet treat is so
amazingly good for you!

## SERVES 2

## TIPS

If you don't have coconut nectar, you can substitute raw honey,
maple syrup or rice syrup. Also, if you're out of vanilla pods, use
¼ teaspoon of pure vanilla powder. Coconut cream is full-cream
coconut milk (it is thicker and contains more coconut fats).

# FIG AND OAT GOODNESS

PICTURED ON PAGE 66 →

**I love figs, dates, oats and spices, so I just had to come up with a smoothie combo that included them all. This one has awesome fibre and minerals from the dried fruit, not to mention the antioxidants from adding spices. If you're into spicy things like chai tea, then this will rock your socks!**

Throw everything except the topping ingredients into your blender and process until silky and smooth (about 60 seconds). Pour into bowls (or glasses if you've thinned it a bit) and sprinkle with the extra pecans, oats, figs and dates. Top it off with a drizzle of maple syrup and a lucky shake of cinnamon. Unbeatable!

## SERVES 2

## TIPS

Don't worry if you don't have time to soak the pecans, it won't affect the texture or taste (it just activates the nuts so the nutrients get into your system faster). And if you prefer your smoothie in a glass, add another cup of almond milk.

2 frozen bananas
90 g (½ cup) dried figs
80 g (½ cup) dried pitted dates
100 g (1 cup) rolled oats
30 g (¼ cup) pecans, soaked and rinsed
pinch ground nutmeg
½ teaspoon ground cinnamon
2 tablespoons maple syrup
750 ml (3 cups) almond milk

### TOPPING

2 tablespoons pecans, chopped
2 tablespoons rolled oats
2 dried figs, roughly chopped
2 dried dates, pitted and roughly chopped
maple syrup, to serve
ground cinnamon, to serve

## STRAWBERRY-ROSE SMOOTHIE

### TIPS

If you can't find edible rose petals, use some of the little petals in rose tea. Rosewater should be easy to find in delicatessens and health food stores.

## CLUB TROPICANA

### TIP

Adding spinach to your smoothie won't dramatically change the flavour, just increase the nutrients!

## FIG AND OAT GOODNESS
SEE PAGE 65

# CLUB TROPICANA

Smoothies are an easy way to get loads of nutrients without sacrificing fibre content, plus they are so quick to prepare. (Sometimes when I practise yoga in the evenings I'm too 'yoga stoned' to cook when I get home, so I whip up a smoothie and that's my dinner done in 5 minutes!) This one is super summery, and is great to make when pineapples and mangoes are in season.

Place the coconut water, coconut oil, banana, pineapple, mango and spinach (if using) in your blender and process until silky smooth. Pour into glasses and sprinkle chia seeds over the top. Ta da!

SERVES 2

500 ml (2 cups) coconut water
2 tablespoons coconut oil
1 frozen banana
230 g (1 cup) chopped pineapple
200 g (1 cup) chopped mango
40 g (1 cup) baby spinach leaves, optional
1 tablespoon chia seeds, to serve

# STRAWBERRY-ROSE SMOOTHIE

This is just gorgeous — a little bit fancy but so worth it! Brazil nut milk is lovely in this one, too, though it can be a little tricky to find (if you have a good processor, try making your own).

Place the strawberries, cashews, rosewater, vanilla seeds, raw honey and almond milk in your blender and process until smooth (this will smell amazing!). Pour into glasses and top with a few rose petals. A fun, girly creation!

SERVES 2

125 g (1 cup) strawberries, fresh or frozen
75 g (½ cup) cashews, soaked and rinsed
1 teaspoon rosewater
½ vanilla pod, split and scraped
2 tablespoons raw honey
500 ml (2 cups) almond milk
edible rose petals, to serve

# GREEN SPEEDIE

1 avocado
2 frozen bananas
40 g (1 cup) baby spinach
 leaves
40 g (1 cup) mint leaves
40 g (1 cup) coriander leaves
 and stalks
500 ml (2 cups) coconut
 water

**This is one of the quickest and easiest ways to get more greens into your diet. It's a beauty for breakfast, lunch or even dinner. It will keep for about 3 days (though will discolour slightly without affecting the flavour) so make a big batch (double the ingredients) and each day top it with something different, such as goji berries, shredded coconut, bee pollen, raw honey, or even a few dollops of almond butter — the list goes on!**

Pop the lot in your blender and whizz until silky smooth (add more coconut water if it's too thick for you — I love to eat mine with a spoon). Now top with your favourite goodies. I like shredded coconut, goji berries and bee pollen. A teaspoon of rolled oats is really nice, too.

SERVES 2

# BANANAMACARAMA

2 frozen bananas
4 medjool dates, pitted
80 g (½ cup) macadamia nuts
2 tablespoons chia seeds,
 optional
½ teaspoon ground cinnamon
pinch ground nutmeg
500 ml (2 cups) almond milk
½ banana, sliced lengthways
 into slivers
pinch ground cinnamon,
 to serve

**Bananas and macadamias are two of my favourite foods, so it's lucky I live in Australia where we grow loads of both! Macadamia nuts are high in fibre, calcium and monounsaturated fats (the good guys), and make excellent brain food.**

Place the bananas, dates, nuts, seeds, spices and almond milk into the blender and process until smooth. Pour into glasses and top with fresh banana slivers and a pinch of cinnamon. Yum!

SERVES 2

TIPS

If macadamias aren't your thing, this recipe works really well with cashews. And if you don't want to use dates, substitute with 2 tablespoons of raw honey, coconut nectar or maple syrup, or 3 drops of stevia.

# SUPER THICK GREENIE

I *love* green smoothies, but for me the texture is everything — they have to be really smooth. I also love eating them from a bowl because it's just a fun way to eat them, so I often make mine quite thick.

Blend all the ingredients together until you get a thick, smooth consistency and all the lumpy bits are gone. Then pour into a big bowl and top with the shredded coconut, goji berries, cashews and bee pollen (if using) — a masterpiece!

## SERVES 2

## TIP

You can use any kind of date for this recipe, but medjools are juicier and sweeter — I reckon they taste like caramel.

This is one of my all-time favourite green smoothies!

2 frozen bananas

100 g (1 cup) rolled oats

80 g (2 cups) baby spinach leaves

2 tablespoons coconut oil, melted

75 g (½ cup) cashews, soaked and rinsed

45 g (¼ cup) medjool dates, pitted

pinch cayenne pepper

½ teaspoon ground cinnamon

## TOPPING

15 g (¼ cup) shredded coconut

30 g (¼ cup) goji berries

1 tablespoon roughly chopped cashews

2 tablespoons bee pollen, optional

# LAVENDER-BLUEBERRY SMOOTHIE

PICTURED OPPOSITE →

300 g (2 cups) blueberries,
  fresh or frozen
2 tablespoons chia seeds
80 g (½ cup) macadamia nuts
2 tablespoons coconut
  nectar
2 tablespoons coconut oil
500 ml (2 cups) coconut
  water
1 teaspoon chia seeds,
  to serve
pinch dried lavender

**I know this one sounds really fancy pants, but it looks so pretty and tastes so incredible that I just had to share it with you! The dried lavender I use is actually organic lavender tea made from a pure, food-grade lavender. It's a wonderful calmative, and is sometimes used to treat insomnia.**

Place the blueberries, chia seeds, macadamias, coconut nectar, coconut oil and coconut water in your blender and process until creamy smooth. Pour into tall glasses and top with the extra chia seeds and a pinch of lavender.

SERVES 2

# CHAI AND ALMOND BUTTER SMOOTHIE

1 frozen banana
4 medjool dates, pitted
2 tablespoons almond butter
½ teaspoon chai spice mix
500 ml (2 cups) almond milk
extra chai spice mix, to serve
1 teaspoon chopped
  almonds, to serve

**By now, you've probably figured out that I have a thing for spices, and this smoothie is no exception! Spices stimulate our circulatory system, which helps to warm us up — perfect in winter.**

Pop the banana, dates, almond butter, spices and almond milk in your blender and whizz till smooth. Pour into glasses and serve topped with a pinch of chai spice and a sprinkle of chopped almonds.

SERVES 2

TIP
If you can't find any chai spice mix, make your own using my recipe on page 94.

# CHOCO-NUT SMOOTHIE

1 frozen banana
4 medjool dates, pitted
150 g (1 cup) cashews,
   soaked and rinsed
2 tablespoons desiccated
   coconut
35 g (¼ cup) cacao powder
2 tablespoons coconut oil
500 ml (2 cups) coconut
   water
shredded coconut, to serve

## TIP
Feel free to swap the dates for
2 tablespoons of maple syrup,
raw honey or coconut nectar,
or 3 drops of stevia.

**Chocolate and coconut — another match made in heaven! Some people freak out when I tell them how much coconut oil I consume a day, but I can promise you this is healthy stuff. Yes, it's a saturated fat, but it's a medium-chain saturated fat so the body uses it for energy rather than storing it. Plus your skin glows and your hair feels soft and luscious — an added bonus!**

Place the banana, dates, cashews, coconut, cacao, coconut oil and coconut water in the blender and process until silky. Pour into glasses, top with a sprinkle of shredded coconut and enjoy this coconut–chocolate masterpiece!

SERVES 2

# CAROB HALVA GOODNESS

2 frozen bananas
2 tablespoons hulled tahini
½ teaspoon ground cinnamon
2 tablespoons carob powder
2 tablespoons raw honey
500 ml (2 cups) almond milk
2 teaspoons sesame seeds,
   to serve
pinch ground cinnamon,
   to serve

**When it comes to smoothies I often used hulled tahini so the flavour isn't too overpowering, but you can use unhulled if you want the extra fibre and nutrients. This recipe uses carob powder, which is another goodie that doesn't get used enough. It's also a great source of fibre and has loads of minerals including magnesium.**

Place the bananas, tahini, cinnamon, carob powder, honey and almond milk in the blender. Process until smooth, pour into glasses and top with sesame seeds and cinnamon. Hashtag yumbo!

SERVES 2

# CHOCOLATE-CHILLI SMOOTHIE

**I just *had* to create a smoothie with my two favourite things: chocolate (with its magnesium and and awesome taste) and chilli (the metabolism booster and cardio-support spice). Give it a try!**

Place the bananas, almond butter, cacao, cayenne, honey and almond milk into the blender. Process until lovely and smooth. Pour into glasses and top with a sprinkle of cacao powder and the tiniest pinch of chilli flakes — if you're game!

SERVES 2

2 frozen bananas
2 tablespoons almond butter
25 g (¼ cup) cacao powder
¼ teaspoon cayenne pepper
2 tablespoons raw honey
500 ml (2 cups) almond milk
extra cacao powder, to serve
chilli flakes, optional

# CHOCOLATE MONKEY MAGIC

**This smoothie almost tastes like dessert, it's *that* good!**

Pop everything into the blender, process until smooth, pour into glasses and you're good to go!

SERVES 2

2 frozen bananas
25 g (¼ cup) cacao powder
4 medjool dates, pitted
500 ml (2 cups) almond milk

TIPS

When freezing your bananas, remember to peel them first! Trust me: it's no fun trying to peel a frozen banana — you end up losing most it because it's stuck to the skin. Also, if you don't fancy dates, use 2 tablespoons of maple syrup, coconut nectar or raw honey, or 3 drops of stevia.

# BERRY AND MINT GRANITA

2 cups frozen berries
20 g (1 cup) mint leaves
2 tablespoons raw honey
2 cups ice cubes
mint sprigs, to serve

## TIP

This also tastes delicious if
you use coconut nectar, maple
syrup, 4 dates, or 3 drops of
stevia instead of raw honey.

**Just four ingredients make up this magical drink. Use any mix of frozen berries you like, or even just one type if you prefer. I love this after a workout, or on a hot summer's day.**

Place the berries, mint leaves, honey and ice in the blender. Process until it looks like a Slurpee. Then pour it into little bowls or glasses, top with a mint sprig and enjoy. I use a spoon when I eat this creation!

## SERVES 2

# THE GREENI YOGINI

2 frozen bananas
1 avocado
80 g (2 cups) baby spinach
  leaves
1 tablespoon goji berries
½ teaspoon ground cinnamon
¼ teaspoon ground nutmeg
3 drops stevia
2 tablespoons coconut oil
500–750 ml (2–3 cups)
  coconut water
1 tablespoon chia seeds,
  to serve
goji berries, to serve
1 tablespoon shredded
  coconut, to serve
extra pinch ground cinnamon,
  to serve

**I created this recipe for my mate, Amy, who runs an awesome Bikram yoga studio here in Melbourne. For me, yoga and eating nourishing food help me to become the best version of myself that I can be, so this delicious, nutrient-dense smoothie is the perfect post-yoga meal!**

Pop your bananas, avocado, spinach, berries, spices, stevia, coconut oil and coconut water into a powerful blender and process until smooth (about 40–60 seconds). Pour into glasses or bowls and top with chia seeds, goji berries, shredded coconut and a final dusting of cinnamon. Enjoy this blissful health bomb. *Namaste*!

## SERVES 2

## TIP

If you don't like stevia, sweeten with 4 medjool dates or 2 tablespoons of raw honey, maple syrup or coconut nectar.

# VANILLA NECTAR

**Vanilla and coconut might be considered subtle flavours on their own, yet together they are a real delight! Try this one and tell me what you think.**

Place the cashews, vanilla seeds, coconut nectar, coconut milk and coconut water in your blender and process well (this combo will be a little thinner than the other recipes). Pour into glasses, top with chia seeds and enjoy with a drinking straw!

SERVES 2

75 g (½ cup) cashews
½ vanilla pod, split and
  scraped
2 tablespoons coconut nectar
375 ml (1½ cups) coconut milk
500 ml (2 cups) coconut water
1 tablespoon chia seeds

TIP
If you don't have coconut nectar, you can use the same quantity of raw honey, maple syrup or rice syrup.

# APPLE, LIME AND MINTIE

**This recipe is a ripper! It keeps well in the fridge for about three days, so you could double the quantities to make enough for a few days' brekkies for yourself or to share.**

Place the apple, avocado, mint, dates and lime juice in your blender with 2 cups of water. Process until smooth. (If you find it too thick, just add a little more water.) Serve in a glass topped with fresh lime zest and a sprig of mint. Yum!

SERVES 2

TIP
I use medjool dates, but if you want to use regular dried dates, soften them by soaking in ½ cup of water or fresh apple juice first (sometimes I even throw this date juice in the combo too!).

1 Granny Smith apple, skin
  left on, roughly chopped
1 avocado
20 g (1 cup) mint leaves
4 medjool dates, pitted
juice and zest of ½ lime
mint sprigs, to serve

# JUICES

For juices to be at their most nutritious, they need to be made with a high-powered juicer that can handle the whole fruit (flesh, skin and all). If you just squeeze the juice out, and leave the flesh and skin behind, you're getting mostly fruit sugar, and not much of any other benefits. Now I know these can cost a bit, but I learned my lesson by buying several cheaper ones and breaking them all!

Keep the skins on apples, pears, carrots, beets, cucumbers, kiwi fruit, lemons, limes and oranges if your juicer can handle it. All you need to do is trim stalks or woody parts and wash them. (I don't core apples or pears.) Also, try to use organic fruits and veggies if possible. If they're not organic, give them a really good wash — some people suggest washing them in water with a splash of apple cider vinegar to help remove any chemical residues. Of course there are some fruit and veggies where it's not a good idea to eat the skins (I'm thinking bananas, pineapples etc.)!

## ALKALIZE ME

160 g (4 cups) kale
160 g (4 cups) baby
   spinach leaves
2 cucumbers
2 Granny Smith apples
40 g (1 cup) mint leaves

## CITRUS BOOSTER

1 grapefruit
2 oranges
1 whole lemon
1 × 2 cm piece ginger

## DETOX

2 carrots
4 stalks celery
1 whole lemon
50 g (1 cup) parsley
1 × 2 cm piece ginger

## ENERGY

3 carrots
2 beets
2 stalks celery
1 × 2 cm piece ginger

## GREEEEN

160 g (4 cups) baby
   spinach leaves
2 cucumbers
4 stalks celery
1 whole lemon
1 whole lime
20 g (½ cup) mint leaves
1 × 2 cm piece ginger

## LIVER CLEANSER

2 carrots
1 large grapefruit
1 whole lemon
1 × 2 cm piece ginger

## SKIN GLOWER

3 carrots
4 kiwi fruits
1 whole lime

Each of these recipes should make 1 mega-sized juice or 2 medium-sized juices (give or take a bit).

Snacks are where we all tend to fall off the wagon, so making sure we have healthy ones to hand is really important to keep us on track. You see, we need to have snacks to keep our metabolism running high, but if we snack on unhealthy stuff it can be enough to undo all of our hard work. So, it's about snacking often but being super smart about it.

Someone once told me it's easier to be healthy than it is to be unhealthy and I didn't believe them, because we have such easy access to tempting junk food. But I've come to realise that healthy snacks are just as easy to find: carrots, nuts, a yummy dip. The sky's the limit — you just have to see that.

Many of the recipes in this section are also perfect as starters when you're having friends over for a meal, so I will give serving sizes as a range, usually from 2 (a mid-morning or mid-afternoon snack) to 4 or more (when sharing as a starter).

# SNACKS

# SPICY RAW SWEET POTATO STACKS

1 large sweet potato, washed
  and thinly sliced
250 g (2 cups) cherry
  tomatoes, finely diced
15 g (½ cup) coriander leaves,
  chopped
2 red chillies, finely diced,
  optional
juice of 1 lime
2 tablespoons olive oil
pinch ground nutmeg
salt
freshly ground black pepper
1 avocado
extra coriander leaves,
  to serve

## TIP
A mandolin slicer comes in
really handy with this recipe.

**You won't believe me until you try this, but raw sweet potato
is really delicious! It makes a great base texture in this
dish, and I keep the skin on so you're getting more of those
antioxidant goodies. Kemi, my friend and raw food guru, first
introduced me to the raw sweet potato with this recipe, and
now I'm hooked!**

Arrange your sweet spud slices on a large serving plate. In a
bowl combine the cherry tomatoes, coriander, chillies (if using),
lime juice, olive oil and nutmeg and season to taste. Spread
each sweet spud slice with a generous scoop of avocado, top
with a teaspoon of spicy salsa and a few leaves of coriander.
Now sit back and watch these little goodies get demolished!

SERVES 2-4

# RAW SPICY NUT MIX

50 g (½ cup) walnuts

80 g (½ cup) Brazil nuts

70 g (½ cup) shelled
  pistachios

3 tablespoons sunflower
  seeds

3 tablespoons pumpkin seeds

½ teaspoon paprika

1 teaspoon chilli flakes,
  optional

salt

freshly ground black pepper

**This is my favourite nut mix. It's got veggo protein, good fats, a few carbs and lots of minerals — *so* much better for you than a packet of potato chips. And if there's a nut in this mix that you don't like, simply swap it for one you do. Easy!**

Combine all your goodies in a bowl, mix well and divvy up into containers. Snacks sorted!

MAKES 6 SERVES

# FROZEN BANANA TREATS

**This is the ultimate study snack. It is *so* easy to make and tastes like mouthfuls of ice cream! When I was studying late at night and stressed out, these little beauties gave me the energy to power on and finish all those essays! The seeds and nuts have good fats and protein, the spices get your circulation going, and the bananas' natural sweetness gives you a hit of energy — all good!**

Place the diced bananas on a tray lined with baking paper and freeze for 2–3 hours. When they're frozen, top each with about ½ teaspoon tahini and lightly dust with cinnamon and nutmeg. Now for the fun part: sprinkle a few of them with sesame seeds, a few with goji berries and the rest with chopped almonds. (That way you get to try different combos and find your favourites.) Eat them while they're still frozen — they taste like little bits of ice cream heaven!

SERVES 1–2

2 bananas, diced
2 tablespoons unhulled tahini
½ teaspoon ground cinnamon
¼ teaspoon ground nutmeg
sesame seeds, to serve
goji berries, to serve
chopped almonds, to serve

TIPS

Unhulled tahini has more nutrients, but a nuttier flavour, so use hulled if you prefer (or any nut butter for that matter — they are all delicious with narnies). When dusting with spices, be careful not to go too crazy with them, as their flavour can be overpowering. The best way is to dust from a height.

# CRISPY KALE CHIPS

750 g kale, washed, stems removed and cut into rough chunks
1 teaspoon paprika
1 teaspoon chilli flakes
2 tablespoons coconut oil, melted
salt
freshly ground black pepper

## TIP

The quantity above is about two big bunches, but by the time you remove the stems and cook it, it won't seem so huge (kale shrinks heaps during cooking).

**Kale (sometimes called Tuscan cabbage) is the king of leafy greens. It's from the brassica family, which includes broccoli and cabbage, and is a top source of magnesium, fibre, iron, vitamin K and calcium — a true powerhouse veggie. Some people say they don't like the taste of kale, but I haven't met many who don't like the taste of these bad boys!**

Preheat the oven to 180°C.

Line a large tray with baking paper and scatter your kale over it. Sprinkle with paprika and chilli flakes, drizzle over the melted coconut oil and season to taste with salt and pepper. Bake in the oven for 10 minutes. You won't believe how light and crispy they are! Store leftovers (if you've got any!) in an airtight container.

## SERVES 4-6

## BASIL PESTO

### TIP
This freezes really well, so you can whip up a mega batch and freeze it in small containers for snacks-on-the-go.

## CORIANDER PESTO

### TIP
Store in a screw-top jar in the fridge (add a little layer of olive oil on top to prevent oxidation). It freezes well, too.

# BASIL PESTO WITH CARROT AND CAPSICUM DIPPERS

**This dip is dairy-free, fresh, nourishing, and bursting with flavour (unlike many store-bought dips which are full of sugar, salt and preservatives). Use it as a snack, as an appetiser when you have friends for dinner, or as a delicious side with fish or meat.**

Place the basil, spinach, garlic, macadamias and oil in your food processor and season to taste. Process until the nuts and greens are combined into a delicious paste — the longer you blend it, the smoother it will get. (I love a chunky paste with a bit of crunch, so I only do it for about 5–10 seconds.) Serve in a dipping bowl on a platter, surrounded by colourful carrot and capsicum dippers.

SERVES 4-8

60 g (2 cups) basil leaves
60 g (1½ cups) baby spinach
    leaves
2 garlic cloves
80 g (½ cup) macadamia nuts
250 ml (1 cup) macadamia
    nut oil
salt
freshly ground black pepper
2 carrots, cut into batons
1 red capsicum, cut into
    batons
1 yellow capsicum, cut
    into batons

# CORIANDER PESTO WITH VEGGIE CHIP DIPPERS

**This pesto recipe is perfect for people with both dairy and nut allergies, and works really well with basil, too. (People with fructose absorption issues should drop the garlic.)**

Preheat the oven to 180°C. Place the sweet potato and parsnip on a baking paper–lined oven tray. Toss them with coconut oil and season to taste. Sprinkle with fennel seeds and bake for 10–15 minutes (watch that they don't burn).

Pop the remaining ingredients except the chia seeds into the food processor and let it work its magic. Place in a pretty serving bowl. When the chippies are done, remove from the oven, sprinkle with chia seeds and allow to cool. It's dipping time!

SERVES 4-8

1 parsnip, very finely sliced
1 small sweet potato, very
    finely sliced
1 tablespoon coconut oil, melted
salt
freshly ground black pepper
1 teaspoon fennel seeds
160 g (4 cups) coriander
    leaves and stalks, chopped
120 g (3 cups) baby spinach
    leaves
250 ml (1 cup) olive oil
juice of 3 lemons
2 garlic cloves
1 teaspoon chia seeds

# CARROT AND CORIANDER DIP

4 carrots, roughly chopped
75 g (½ cup) cashews, soaked
  (overnight if possible,
  otherwise for 20 minutes)
  and rinsed
125 ml (½ cup) olive oil
25 g (½ cup) coriander
  leaves and stalks, roughly
  chopped
120 g (1 cup) cherry tomatoes
sea salt, to taste
freshly ground black pepper,
  to taste
thinly sliced radishes, to
  serve (or veggie chip
  dippers, see page 89)

**Carrots are jam-packed with fibre and vitamins. They also contain beta-carotene which is converted to vitamin A (an important nutrient for eye health). Carrot sticks can get pretty boring after a while, but this dip turns the humble carrot into something pretty special!**

Pop all the ingredients except the radishes into a high-powered processor and blend until nice and smooth. Serve with thinly sliced radish dippers.

## SERVES 4–8

## TIPS

Use a high-powered processor for this, as carrots are quite fibrous. (If you don't have a super gutsy processor, first pulse your ingredients for 3–4 minutes so you don't burn your motor out, or grate your carrots first.) And use your whole bunch of coriander (the leaves, stalks and roots) as most of the flavour is in the stems and roots. (Wash it well, of course.)

# SPICY ROAST PUMPKIN DIP

**I love this creation! It not only tastes unreal on its own, but makes an awesome replacement for mashed spuds. Try it with some lamb cutlets and a handful of greens, or toss it with raw zucchini pasta for a whole new meal.**

Preheat the oven to 180°C.

Spread the pumpkin on a baking tray, drizzle with coconut oil, sprinkle with caraway seeds and season. Bake for 30–40 minutes, or until pumpkin is soft. Allow to cool slightly before blending in a food processor until smooth. Serve garnished with a sprinkle of caraway seeds.

SERVES 4–8

TIPS

You can use any type of pumpkin for this. The dip freezes well, and will last for 4 days in the fridge.

400 g (3 cups) roughly chopped pumpkin
2 teaspoons coconut oil, melted
1 teaspoon caraway seeds
salt, to taste
freshly ground black pepper, to taste
extra caraway seeds, to serve

# RAW CHOC-BERRY NUT MIX

80 g (½ cup) macadamia nuts

30 g (½ cup) shredded
  coconut

3 tablespoons cacao nibs

60 g (½ cup) goji berries

80 g (½ cup) almonds

3 tablespoons pumpkin seeds

3 tablespoons dried
  cranberries

½ teaspoon ground cinnamon

**Being healthy means being organised, so if crappy snacks are
your biggest downfall, keep a container of this sweet nut mix
in your bag for when you're doing a zillion and one things and
need a little pick-me-up!**

Place everything in a bowl, mix well then divide between six
little containers ready for snacking!

MAKES 6 SERVES

# HOMEMADE CHAI MIX

2 tablespoons ground
cinnamon

2 tablespoons crushed
cardamom seeds

3 tablespoons ground
turmeric

1 teaspoon ground cloves

2 tablespoons ground ginger

## TIP

Although this lasts for yonks,
I prefer mine fresh, so I usually
make a fresh batch every
couple of weeks.

**This chai mix is a spicy antioxidant goldmine! It's totally
caffeine free, so you can use it to brew an almond-milk chai,
or you could add it to a black tea or liquorice tea base. I even
add this little combo to my porridge, smoothies, slices, muffins
and cakes.**

Combine the spices in a sealable glass jar and store in the
pantry to use as required.

MAKES ABOUT 100 G

# WORLD'S BEST AVO MASH

**I've had loads of practice making avocado mash, and I think this is the absolute best way to do it! You can use it as a dip or as a side for any meal (it goes beautifully with spicy roo fillet and roast tomatoes, for example).**

Halve and stone the avocados. Scoop the flesh into a large bowl. Add the lime juice, chilli, coriander, cumin, salt and pepper and mix well. Serve with whatever takes your fancy. My all-time favourite way to eat it is with spicy tomato and chilli salsa (see page 82) and with raw sweet potato slices as my dippers. Yumbo!

SERVES 2–4

2 large avocados
juice of 1 lime
1 red chilli, finely chopped
50 g (1 cup) chopped
   coriander leaves
**pinch ground cumin**
**salt, to taste**
**freshly ground black pepper,**
   **to taste**

I'm not going to go on about the nutritional value of veggies (we all know how awesome they are), but I do want to say that nutritionally, raw food is the bee's knees — whenever I can, I will eat my veggies and fruit uncooked.

Loading up on fresh fruit and veggies at a local farmers market is one of my *favourite* things! I'm a massive fan of organic and biodynamic produce, as it's been farmed without artificial chemicals and genetically modified materials. (Biodynamic certification guidelines are actually stricter than those required for organic certification, demanding a holistic system that protects the vitality of the plants, soil and/or livestock and using preparations made from minerals and herbs — similar to homeopathy — to enhance the compost applied to the fields.)

Most of the meals in this section can be served as a main dish, or as a side. If you serve them as a side, the quantity will go further (usually serving twice as many), though it depends on how hungry everyone is!

Green salad leaves are a big part of all my recipes, veggo recipes in particular, and it's always important to dry your salad leaves so they can soak up the flavours of the dressing — water-logged salads are sloppy and just don't taste as good.

# VEGAN
## AND
# VEGGIE
# DISHES

# QUINOA SUPERFOOD SALAD

400 g (2 cups) quinoa, rinsed
pinch salt
250 g broccoli florets, finely
   chopped
½ red onion, finely sliced
130 g (1 cup) shelled
   pistachios, roughly chopped
1 large beetroot, grated
250 g (2 cups) cherry
   tomatoes, quartered
60 g (½ cup) goji berries
1 pomegranate
3 tablespoons olive oil
juice and zest of 1 lemon
salt
freshly ground black pepper
mint sprigs, to serve

## TIPS

I use a mix of all black, white
and red quinoa, but it works
really well with just the red
variety. Also, feel free to use
the broccoli stalks as they're
full of nutrients and fibre.
(I only leave them out when
cooking for my mates as the
salad looks a lot prettier.)
Leftovers are delicious for
lunch (just store in an airtight
container in the fridge).

**I love quinoa. It's a great source of plant protein, is gluten-free and although technically a seed, works beautifully as a replacement for grains. It's got a delicious nutty taste and a texture a bit like couscous, and is the perfect base for this super-colourful superfood salad.**

Place the rinsed quinoa in a saucepan with 4 cups of water and a pinch of salt, cover and bring to the boil. Reduce the heat and simmer for 10–15 minutes, covered, until cooked. (You'll know when it's ready because it will triple in size and appear to have sprouted little 'tails'. It should look nice and fluffy, not gluggy.) Remove from the heat and place in a large serving bowl. Immediately add the broccoli and onion and mix it through (the heat from the quinoa will slightly soften the veggies). Add the pistachios, beetroot, cherry toms and goji berries, and mix well.

Cut the pomegranate in half and with the side of a heavy knife tap the seeds out into the mix and stir through your colourful creation, squeezing any pomegranate juice over the top.

Then in a little bowl whisk together the olive oil, lemon juice and zest and season to taste. Pour over the salad and top with a few sprigs of mint.

SERVES 4–6

# PUMPKIN SOUP WITH CASHEW CREAM

700 g (6 cups) roughly
  chopped pumpkin
120 ml (½ cup) coconut oil
1 heaped teaspoon cumin
  seeds
1 heaped teaspoon chilli flakes
1 brown onion, diced
2 garlic cloves, finely diced
2 teaspoons yellow curry
  paste
1.5 litres (6 cups) vegetable
  stock
salt
freshly ground black pepper
300 g (2 cups) cashews,
  soaked and rinsed
extra chilli flakes, for cashew
  cream
3 tablespoons pumpkin
  seeds, to serve
extra olive oil, to serve

## TIPS

You should be able to find
yellow curry paste easily; it's
milder than green or red curry
pastes, and is used heaps in
Indian cooking. And try to
soak your cashews for at least
an hour — it helps digestion.

**This is a dairy-free, vegan and paleo-friendly creation. The cashews give an awesome creaminess to the naturally sweet and smooth texture of pumpkin!**

Preheat the oven to 180°C.

Place the pumpkin on a baking tray and spread 4 tablespoons of the coconut oil over the pumpkin pieces. (I know it's going to be solid at room temperature, so use a teaspoon to put dobs here and there. It'll melt as soon as it's in the oven.) Sprinkle over the cumin seeds and chilli flakes. Bake for 20–30 minutes, until the pumpkin is soft.

Heat the remaining coconut oil (about 2 tablespoons) in a large saucepan over a medium heat. Add the onion and cook until translucent. Throw in the garlic and curry paste and cook for another minute to release the flavours. Add the roast pumpkin (juices and all), vegetable stock and mix. Cover and bring to the boil. Reduce heat and simmer for 20 minutes. Season to taste. Blend with a hand-held processor until it's nice and smooth (if you don't have one of these you can pour the mixture into a big processor, but it can get messy). Set aside to cool slightly.

Drain the cashews, place them in the food processor with 2 cups of water and blend until smooth. You can serve your cashew cream just like this, but I love to tweak it with a smidge of salt, pepper and chilli flakes, then give it one more whizz before pouring it into a little jug.

Serve the soup with a generous swirl of cashew cream, a sprinkle of pumpkin seeds, one last hit of freshly ground black pepper and a drizzle of olive oil.

SERVES 6

# MANGO, AVOCADO AND MACADAMIA SALAD

**This summery salad is perfect for any occasion, from a cruisy barbecue to a fancy dinner party. Another vegan delight, its amazing fats are excellent brain- and mood-boosters.**

Lightly roast the macadamias on a low heat in a small frying pan for 1–2 minutes, shaking the pan so they toast evenly (you won't need to add any oil as they will release their own).

Place the mango, avocado and macadamias in a large bowl and mix. Add the chilli and onion and stir through gently. Lastly, add the rocket (make sure it's dry so it can soak up all the amazing flavours) and give it a very light toss with your fingers.

In a small jug or bowl, whisk together the lime juice, lime zest, olive oil, mustard, honey and garlic. Season to taste. Pour the dressing over the salad and toss lightly with your fingertips so it coats everything but doesn't bruise the rocket leaves. Then enjoy this amazing flavour bomb!

SERVES 4–6

160 g (1 cup) macadamia nuts
2 large mangoes, cubed
2 large avocados, diced
1–2 red chillies, finely sliced
1 red onion, finely sliced
150 g (5 cups) rocket, washed and dried
juice and zest of 1 lime
80 ml (⅓ cup) olive oil
1 tablespoon wholegrain mustard
2 tablespoons raw honey, melted
1 garlic clove, crushed
pink salt
freshly ground black pepper

TIP
If you don't fancy it hot then just use one chilli.

# BUCKWHEAT CREPES WITH SPINACH AND RICOTTA

**This is a yummy gluten-free recipe, and perfect to serve to mates for lunch. Don't be confused by the name. Buckwheat doesn't contain any wheat. In fact, it's not even a grain. It's actually the seed of a plant related to the rhubarb family. It's high in bioflavonoids, which increase blood flow and help the body absorb vitamin C, just to name a few benefits. I know the raisins might sound like a weird addition, but they bring a touch of sweetness that makes the world of difference!**

Place the pine nuts in a small frying pan over a medium heat for a couple of minutes, shaking the pan so they brown evenly (they contain lots of oil so will burn easily if you don't keep an eye on them). Set them aside.

Combine the ricotta, spinach, red onion and toasted pine nuts in a bowl and season to taste. (Preparing the filling first means it's ready to go when you've made your crepes.)

Place the eggs and almond milk in a bowl or large jug and stir well. In a mixing bowl combine the buckwheat flour, salt and pepper. Make a well in the centre and gradually add the egg and milk mixture, stirring in little circles so you catch the flour from around the edges (this stops you getting big clumps). Continue adding the liquid and mixing it in until the batter is smooth, like thick milk.

Heat a tablespoon of butter in a frying pan over a medium heat (be careful it doesn't burn). When melted, quickly pour in ¼ cup of the batter, tilting the pan so it spreads evenly to make a nice thin crepe. Cook for 1 minute (or a bit longer if you didn't manage to spread it thinly enough). Use a spatula or palette knife to flip the crepe and cook the other side for a further minute. Set aside on baking paper while you cook the rest.

To serve, place generous spoonfuls of filling into the centre of each crepe, roll up, sprinkle with a few raisins and enjoy!

SERVES 4–6

3 tablespoons pine nuts
250 g (1 cup) ricotta
80 g (2 cups) baby spinach leaves, finely chopped
1 small red onion, finely diced
salt
freshly ground black pepper
2 eggs, lightly beaten
600 ml almond milk
300 g (2 cups) buckwheat flour, sifted
butter, for frying
3 tablespoons raisins

TIP
Toasting pine nuts releases their flavour, but you can still use them raw, too.

# ROCKET, MACADAMIA AND STRAWBERRY SALAD

120 g (4 cups) rocket, rinsed
  and dried
250 g (2 cups) strawberries,
  hulled and quartered
2 large avocados, diced
160 g (1 cup) macadamia
  nuts, roughly chopped
3 tablespoons olive oil
1 tablespoon balsamic
  vinegar
salt
freshly ground black pepper

**This bright, antioxidant-dense detox salad is easy to whip up, makes an awesome side salad and is also a great vegan meal on its own.**

Place the rocket, strawbs, avocado and macadamia nuts in a large bowl and gently toss with your fingers.

In a small bowl or jug whisk together the olive oil and balsamic vinegar, and season to taste. Pour the dressing over the salad and toss. Now enjoy your nourishing creation!

SERVES 2

# QUICK KALE AND SILVERBEET

**Green leafy veggies are the bomb when it comes to health. The list of nutrients goes on forever! This veggie powerhouse is a staple for me. I promise you'll be going back for seconds!**

First, toast the pine nuts in a frying pan over a medium heat for a couple of minutes, shaking the pan so they brown evenly. Set aside.

Heat the coconut oil in the pan and sauté the onion for 2 minutes or until translucent. Add the garlic, cooking for another minute, then the allspice and dried cranberries. Stir lightly then add the silverbeet and kale (and chilli if you want it to pack a little less punch) then season to taste. Cook for about 4 minutes. (It will look like loads at first, but the greens reduce rapidly to a quarter of their original size.) Chilli heads can add the chilli just before serving.

Serve with a drizzle of lemon juice, a pinch of zest, a big glug of olive oil, then top with the roasted pine nuts. Yum!

## SERVES 2

## TIPS

Kale also goes by the names Tuscan cabbage or cavolo nero (there are lots of different types: purple, curly, black), but if you can't find any, spinach is just as good. Also, if you're not a chilli fan, add the chilli at the same time as you add the greens to reduce its bite.

2 tablespoons pine nuts
2 tablespoons coconut oil
1 large red onion, finely diced
3 garlic cloves, finely chopped
pinch ground allspice
60 g (½ cup) dried cranberries
400 g silverbeet, washed, stalks removed and roughly chopped
400 g kale, washed, stalks removed and roughly chopped
2 red chillies, finely diced
salt
freshly ground black pepper
juice and zest of 1 lemon
olive oil, to serve

# TWO-MINUTE CHERRY TOMATO AND STRAWBERRY SALAD

**This is so simple, but adds so much flavour to any meal as a side dish that I had to share it with you.**

Combine the tomatoes, strawberries and basil leaves in a serving bowl. Pour over the olive oil and balsamic and season to taste. Toss and enjoy!

SERVES 2

250 g (2 cups) cherry tomatoes, halved
250 g (2 cups) strawberries, hulled and halved
40 g (1 cup, tightly packed) basil leaves, finely chopped
3 tablepoons olive oil
1 tablespoon balsamic vinegar
salt
freshly ground black pepper

# SUPER SPROUT SALAD WITH TAHINI DRESSING

2 teaspoons cumin seeds
125 g (2 cups) mixed sprouts
250 g (2 cups) baby radishes, sliced
1 purple carrot, sliced
1 orange carrot, sliced
250 g (2 cups) cherry tomatoes, halved
30 g (1 cup) coriander leaves, roughly chopped
30 g (1 cup) flat-leaf parsley leaves, roughly chopped
1 garlic clove, crushed
3 tablespoons olive oil
2 tablespoons unhulled tahini
80 ml (⅓ cup) lemon juice
salt
freshly ground black pepper

## TIP
If you can't find purple carrots, just use two orange ones.

**One look at the bright colours in this awesome raw salad and you just know it's good for you! Sprouts have loads of vital enzymes because they're actually *still growing* when you pop them on your plate! And there are so many to choose from. I love mung bean, chickpea, adzuki bean and lentil sprouts, but use whatever you have to hand.**

Toast the cumin seeds in a small frying pan over a medium heat for about 2 minutes, moving them around the pan so they don't burn. When they start to give off an aroma, remove from the heat. Place the seeds in a mortar and crush them to a fine powder using a pestle.

Place the sprouts, radishes, carrots, cherry toms and herbs in a large serving bowl. In another small bowl place the garlic, olive oil, tahini, lemon juice, salt and pepper and whisk to combine. Pour the dressing over the salad and toss it with the tips of your fingers (it's the best way!). Dust with freshly ground cumin and serve. Serve this to a mate and make their day!

SERVES 4

# SPICY SWEET POTATOES WITH KALE AND BRAZIL NUTS

**This one is an all-round winner; it's got nut protein and stacks of vitamins, minerals and antioxidants. It's a meal in itself, or a tasty side for a roo steak. Sweet spud and cinnamon are a match made in heaven!**

Preheat the oven to 180°C. Place the whole sweet spuds on a baking tray. Poke each one a few times with a fork then rub each with 1 tablespoon of coconut oil. (The oil will be solid at room temperature, but will melt as soon as it's in the oven.) Roast in the oven for 40–50 minutes. Check at the 20-minute mark and turn over to ensure they cook evenly. When they've got 10 minutes to go, get your kale topper ready.

Place the remaining coconut oil in a frying pan over a medium heat. When melted, add the kale and sauté for 4 minutes. Add the chilli and cook for another minute. Remove from the heat and toss in the Brazil nuts (reserving a teaspoon for garnish).

Pop each sweet spud on a serving plate, slice it in half, and top with half each of the spicy kale mixture and avocado. Garnish with a sprinkle of the remaining Brazil nuts, a drizzle of olive oil and a good pinch of cinnamon.

Devour!

SERVES 2

2 sweet potatoes, washed, skin on
3 tablespoons coconut oil
200 g kale, stalks removed, roughly chopped
1 red chilli, finely diced
70 g (½ cup) roughly chopped Brazil nuts
1 large avocado, diced
olive oil, to serve
pinch ground cinnamon

# QUINOA WRAPS

400 g (2 cups) red quinoa,
  rinsed
2 large avocados, diced
2 red chillies, finely diced
60 g (2 cups) coriander
  leaves, finely chopped
1 large red onion, finely diced
120 g (1 cup) cherry
  tomatoes, halved
40 g (1 cup) baby spinach
  leaves
juice and zest of 1 lime
60 ml (¼ cup) olive oil
salt
freshly ground black pepper
8 nori sheets

## TIP
Leftovers make great lunches
for work. They should last
for 2 days stored in a sealed
container in the fridge.

**Inspired by the lovely feedback I got about the nori wraps in my last book, I wanted to make a new, equally healthy and delicious version. I'm really rapt (sorry!) about this one. Your body will be buzzing after you gobble up these little gems.**

Pop the quinoa into a saucepan with 4 cups of water. Bring it to the boil and simmer, covered, for 10–15 minutes until all the water is absorbed and the quinoa is fluffy (it will have tripled in size and appear to have sprouted little 'tails'). Remove from the heat and transfer to a large mixing bowl. Add the avocado, chilli, coriander, onion, cherry tomatoes and spinach and mix well. Add the lime juice and zest, olive oil and salt and pepper to taste, and give it another toss. Divide it into 8 even portions in the bowl.

Place the first nori sheet on a cutting board or rolling mat (or just a clean surface). Place one portion of the quinoa mixture in a sausage-like shape along the lower edge of the nori sheet (closest to you). Moisten the top edge with a pastry brush dipped in water. Now roll the sheet up gently (away from you). The moistened top edge should be like a little envelope flap, sealing it up.

Repeat with the remaining sheets and quinoa mixture until you have 8 rolls. Munch on some right away!

MAKES 8 WRAPS

# BEST ROAST PUMPKIN

1.5 kg pumpkin, cut into
   2 cm pieces
125 ml (½ cup) coconut oil,
   melted
2 tablespoons maple syrup
½ teaspoon ground cinnamon
½ teaspoon ground nutmeg
pinch salt
70 g (½ cup) pumpkin seeds
60 g (½ cup) dried
   cranberries, to serve

TIP

The sweeter pumpkins such as butternut and jap work best with this recipe.

**I love, *love* this recipe. You can prepare this as a side dish for meat, fish or a big green salad, but it's pretty awesome on its own, too. I hope you like it as much as I do!**

Preheat the oven to 180°C. Place the pumpkin on a large baking tray.

In a small bowl whisk the coconut oil, maple syrup, spices and salt, then drizzle over the pumpkin pieces. If the coconut oil starts to harden before you're done, use your hands to spread it over the pumpkin pieces (the warmth of your hands will keep it soft).

Bake the pumpkin for 20–30 minutes (or a bit longer if your chunks are bigger). Test with a fork (the flesh should be soft, but not mushy). Remove from the oven and quickly sprinkle with the pumpkin seeds. Roast for another 2 minutes. Serve in little bowls and sprinkle with dried cranberries.

SERVES 4–6

# VEGGIE CURRY WITH CREAMY QUINOA

**A spicy veggie curry is the perfect winter warmer, and a delicious way to get a load of phytonutrients (plant nutrients) and antioxidants all in one go. By adding some nuts, you'll get a broad spectrum of amino acids, too, which is important if you're not eating meat. Always make enough so that you have leftovers, as it tastes even better the next day.**

Heat the coconut oil in a large frying pan over a medium heat. Sauté the onion for 2 minutes or until translucent. Add the garlic, celery and ginger and sauté for another minute. Pop in your chickpeas, pumpkin, sweet spud, grated carrot, spices, chilli, salt and pepper along with 1 can of coconut cream and 3 cups of water. Cook on a low heat for 30 minutes.

Meanwhile, place the remaining coconut cream in another saucepan along with 2 cups of water, the desiccated coconut and the quinoa. Bring to the boil, then reduce the heat, cover and simmer for 15 minutes, or until you notice the quinoa has grown to about 3 times its size. Set aside and keep warm.

When the pumpkin and sweet spuds are nice and soft, add the cashews and stir them through. Serve the curry over the coconut quinoa and top with ½ cup coriander leaves and a good squeeze of fresh lime.

## SERVES 4

## TIPS

I use a mix of red, black and white quinoa in this recipe, but any is fine. Also, tinned chickpeas are easy to find, but if you prefer to use dried, soak 1 cup overnight and then cook in fresh water for 1 hour the next morning (this will make 2 cups).

2 tablespoons coconut oil
1 brown onion, diced
2 garlic cloves, finely diced
2 stalks celery, sliced
1 tablespoon grated ginger
2 × 400 g cans chickpeas, drained
240 g (2 cups) cubed pumpkin
280 g (2 cups) cubed sweet potato
1 carrot, grated
¼ teaspoon ground turmeric
½ teaspoon ground cinnamon
½ teaspoon ground cumin
½ teaspoon ground coriander
1 teaspoon mustard seeds
1 red chilli, finely diced
salt
freshly ground black pepper
2 × 400 ml cans coconut cream
2 tablespoons desiccated coconut
400 g (2 cups) mixed quinoa, rinsed
150 g (1 cup) cashews
60 g (2 cups) coriander leaves, roughly chopped
juice of 1 lime

# FRESH FARMERS MARKET SALAD

80 g (2 cups) baby spinach
   leaves, washed and dried
250 g (2 cups) heirloom
   cherry tomatoes
1 purple carrot, grated
1 large avocado, diced
50 g (½ cup) walnuts,
   roughly chopped
60 g (½ cup) sunflower seeds
60 g (½ cup) white
   mulberries
80 ml (⅓ cup) olive oil
juice of 1 lemon
chilli flakes, to taste
salt
freshly ground black pepper

**I've named this salad after one of my favourite places — my local farmers market. And remember my rule: if there's something in here you don't like, just swap it for something you love!**

Place your green leaves, tomatoes, carrot, avocado, walnuts, 3 tablespoons of the sunflower seeds and 3 tablespoons of the berries in a large bowl. Toss using your fingertips (you'll get a better mix happening). Add the olive oil, lemon juice, chilli flakes and season to taste. Give it another mix and serve it topped with the remaining sunflower seeds and dried berries. You're set to go!

SERVES 2

TIPS

If you can't find the rainbow-coloured heirloom tomatoes, then use cherry tomatoes. And an ordinary carrot makes a fine replacement for a purple one. If you can't get white mulberries at your health food store, use any dried berry (cranberries, blueberries or goji berries).

# DETOX RAINBOW SALAD WITH ALMOND-BUTTER DRESSING

**Ever have one of those days when you just don't feel 100 per cent? This salad is a nutritional health bomb that will soon have you feeling better! It's perfect as a side or a main, so whether you're a raw food vegan or paleo meat eater, this salad will keep you happy.**

Combine the carrot, apple, rocket, spinach, capsicum, tomatoes, avocado, goji berries, seeds, nuts, coriander and chilli flakes (to taste) in a large bowl and mix well.

Place the almond butter, lemon juice and olive oil in a small jar. Season, replace the lid, and shake well to combine. This dressing is meant to be quite thick, but if you want it runnier add the juice of 1 more lemon and 2 more tablespoons of olive oil. Pour the dressing over the salad and toss.

Serve with a sprinkle of goji berries, pumpkin seeds and sunflower seeds. Talk about nutritious!

## SERVES 4

## TIP

Goji berries can easily be replaced with cranberries, sultanas or raisins, and if you don't have almond butter, use tahini.

1 large carrot, grated
1 Granny Smith apple, grated
80 g (2 cups) rocket, washed and dried
40 g (1 cup) baby spinach leaves, washed and dried
1 red capsicum, roughly diced
120 g (1 cup) cherry tomatoes, halved
1 large avocado, cubed
60 g (½ cup) goji berries
3 tablespoons pumpkin seeds
3 tablespoons sunflower seeds
3 tablespoons almonds
70 g (½ cup) shelled pistachios
30 g (1 cup) coriander leaves, chopped
chilli flakes, to taste
2 tablespoons almond butter
juice of 1 lemon
2 tablespoons olive oil
salt
freshly ground black pepper
extra goji berries, pumpkin seeds and sunflower seeds, to serve

# VEGGIE PIZZA WITH CAULIFLOWER BASE

## CRUST

480 g (4 cups) steamed cauliflower

100 g (1 cup) almond meal

4 eggs, lightly beaten

80 ml (⅓ cup) coconut oil, melted

salt

freshly ground black pepper

chilli flakes, optional

## TOPPING

80 ml (⅓ cup) tomato paste

40 g (1 cup firmly packed) basil leaves, roughly chopped

1 zucchini, thinly sliced

60 g (1 cup) finely chopped broccoli florets

40 g (½ cup) sliced Swiss brown mushrooms

40 g (¼ cup) pitted kalamata olives, roughly chopped

120 g (1 cup) cherry tomatoes, halved

1 red chilli, finely diced

50 g (¼ cup) goat's feta, crumbled, optional

pink salt

freshly ground black pepper

40 g (1 cup) baby spinach leaves

olive oil, to serve

1 tablespoon sunflower seeds

1 tablespoon pumpkin seeds

½ cup sunflower sprouts

**My amazing teacher Randa always said that if a nutritionist has to take a particular kind of food away from a client, they must always offer a replacement. Pizza is one of those wheat- and dairy-based foods that people really miss, so I've created this pizza with a base of blitzed-up cauliflower and almond meal instead.**

Preheat the oven to 180°C. Place the steamed cauliflower in a mixing bowl and mash well (it will look a bit like rice). Mix in the almond meal, eggs, coconut oil and season to taste with salt, pepper and chilli flakes (if using). Divide the mixture between two baking trays greased with a little coconut oil, shaping each into a circle and pressing it out with your fingertips to a thickness of 1–2 cm. Cook the bases for 10 minutes or until the edges start to brown slightly. Remove from the oven (don't worry if they're still a bit mushie in the middle as they'll be cooked again with the toppings).

Spread half the tomato paste evenly over each base (going right to the edges). Sprinkle over the basil (half for each base). Arrange half the zucchini slices on top of each, followed by the broccoli, mushies, olives, cherry tomatoes, chilli and goat's feta (if using). Season to taste, and return to the oven for a further 5–10 minutes.

When cooked, remove from the oven. Place half the spinach on each pizza (it will wilt), drizzle with olive oil and sprinkle with sunflower seeds, pumpkin seeds and fresh sprouts. Eat with a knife and fork. It's deelishimo!

SERVES 4

## TIPS

If you can't find sunflower sprouts, any sprouts will do perfectly well. This is also delicious topped with roasted pumpkin and spinach, but feel free to make up your own combo!

# QUINOA-STUFFED CAPSICUMS

**These little gems are not only easy to whip up, they are also lovely hot or cold. If you're fine with legumes, the black beans are a fast way to up your protein hit.**

Preheat the oven to 180°C.

Heat the coconut oil in a large frying pan over a medium heat. Sauté the onion and celery until they begin to soften. Add the cumin, paprika, garlic and chillies and cook for 2 minutes until fragrant. Stir in the kale and tomatoes. Cook for 5 minutes or until about 2 tablespoons of the liquid has evaporated. Add the black beans, quinoa and grated carrot along with 2 cups of water. Bring to the boil and simmer for 20 minutes or until the quinoa is cooked.

Meanwhile, scoop out the seeds and fleshy ribs of the capsicum halves so they look like little boats and place them in a baking dish. Take half of the goat's cheese and sprinkle it between the six 'boats'. Pour the quinoa mixture into each capsicum half and any remaining liquid into the bottom of the baking dish (now they really do look like little boats!). Cover with foil and bake for 45 minutes.

Remove from the oven, remove the foil and discard. Sprinkle the tops with the remaining goat's feta. Return to the oven (uncovered), and cook for another 15 minutes or until golden on top. Remove from the oven and allow to rest for 5 minutes.

To serve, place 2 capsicum boats on a bed of rocket, drizzle with olive oil and sprinkle with crushed walnuts and a shake of paprika. The perfect veggie meal!

SERVES 6

2 tablespoons coconut oil
1 brown onion, diced
2 celery stalks, thinly sliced
½ teaspoon ground cumin
½ teaspoon paprika
2 garlic cloves, finely diced
2 red chillies, finely diced
160 g (4 cups) roughly chopped kale
2 × 400 g cans diced tomatoes
1 × 425 g can black beans, rinsed, optional
200 g (1 cup) quinoa, rinsed
2 carrots, grated
6 large red capsicums, halved lengthways
200 g (1 cup) goat's feta, crumbled
160 g (4 cups) rocket, washed and dried
olive oil, to serve
125 g (1 cup) crushed walnuts, to serve
paprika, to serve

## TIPS

I prefer red or royal black quinoa because both have a great taste and nutty texture, but it's fine to use white quinoa if that's all you have. Any leafy green veggie works well in this dish.

I'm not a vegetarian, but I *love* veggo meals, and will happily eat them and not feel like I'm missing out. That said, my 20/20 Diet is partly inspired by paleo-eating principles, which means I eat whole, unprocessed foods similar to what our ancestors hunted and gathered for millennia before they settled down and began farming and processing grains and dairy foods. So my diet is rich in seeds, nuts, fruit (especially berries) and vegetables, but it also features fish, poultry, beef, lamb and game. Any meat I eat, however, *must* be ethically produced. So this means certified organic red meat, sustainably sourced fish, and cage-free poultry and eggs. I know this is more expensive, but health is my number one priority so I'm happy to invest in the best quality food. Be careful with product labelling — some producers use the word 'free-range' when, in fact, the birds are still in cages — just slightly bigger ones. If you're not sure that a product is genuinely organic or has been ethically produced, email or call the producer to find out.

# FISH, POULTRY AND MEAT

# CHARLIE'S SALAD WITH CRISPY SALMON

1 Lebanese cucumber, sliced

1 red capsicum, diced

2 large avocados, cubed

120 g (1 cup) cherry
   tomatoes, halved

12 kalamata olives, pitted and
   roughly chopped

60 g (2 cups) coriander
   leaves, roughly chopped

40 g (1 cup tightly packed)
   basil leaves, roughly
   chopped

40 g (1 cup) mint leaves,
   roughly chopped

80 ml (⅓ cup) olive oil

chilli flakes

salt

freshly ground black pepper

2 tablespoons coconut oil

2 × 180 g salmon fillets,
   skin on

**This recipe was created by an amazing friend of mine who helped me through a really tough time. This salad helped me to fall in love with real, nourishing wholefoods again. Charlie, you are one special soul who changed my life. Thank you.**

Combine the cucumber, capsicum, avocado, tomatoes, olives and fresh herbs in a large salad bowl. Pour in the olive oil, season to taste with chilli flakes, salt and pepper, then give it a good toss. Set aside.

Heat the coconut oil in a frying pan over a high heat. Place the salmon fillets in the pan, skin-side down, and cook for 3 minutes if you like it a little rare, 4 minutes if you prefer it cooked more. Flip the fillets and cook for 1 minute more. (The skin should be nice and crispy, but not burnt.)

Divide the salad between two plates, and serve the salmon on top. There's something wonderful about the flavours in this simple dish that will have you hooked from the first mouthful!

SERVES 2

# MACKEREL AND SUPER GREENS WITH YOGHURT DRESSING

**I love sardines, and a British guy I once met told me, 'If you like sardines you have to try mackerel'. So I did, and loved it. It's an oily fish with heaps of omega-3, and a lovely strong flavour.**

Heat 2 tablespoons of the coconut oil in a frying pan over a medium heat. Place the mackerel fillets in the pan and cook for about 2 minutes on each side. Turn off the heat and cover to keep warm.

Heat the remaining coconut oil in another frying pan. Sauté the kale and broccoli until they brighten in colour (about 4 minutes). Remove from the heat and place in a large serving bowl. Add the spinach, sunflower seeds and pumpkin seeds and toss gently.

Combine the yoghurt, lemon juice, mustard and dill in a small bowl or jug and season to taste.

Break the mackerel into small pieces and toss through the green salad. Divide between serving bowls, spoon over the yoghurt dressing, top with a sprig of dill, a drizzle of olive oil and a hit of freshly ground black pepper.

## SERVES 2

## TIP
This is a good one to have for lunch the next day — it tastes just as awesome served cold!

3 tablespoons coconut oil
4 × 100 g mackerel fillets
200 g (5 cups) roughly chopped kale
120 g (2 cups) chopped broccoli
80 g (2 cups) baby spinach leaves
3 tablespoons sunflower seeds
3 tablespoons pumpkin seeds
150 g (½ cup) plain full-cream yoghurt
2 tablespoons lemon juice
2 tablespoons wholegrain mustard
20 g (1 cup) dill leaves, roughly chopped
salt
freshly ground black pepper
dill sprigs, to serve
olive oil, to serve

# CHICKEN SCHNITZEL WITH ROASTED BABY CARROTS

400 g (about 20) baby
  carrots
2 tablespoons maple syrup
80 ml (⅓ cup) coconut oil
1 teaspoon chilli flakes
salt
freshly ground black pepper
4 × 180 g chicken breast
  fillets
2 eggs
125 g (1¼ cups) almond meal
juice and zest of 1 lemon
1 tablespoon flat-leaf parsley
  leaves, finely chopped
2 large avocados, finely sliced
olive oil

## TIP

If you can't find baby carrots
(sometimes called Dutch
carrots), cut a couple of
big dudes into quarters
lengthways — they're just
as tasty!

**Classic chicken schnitzel is not always the healthiest option with its wheat coating and non-fry-safe oils. So here's my healthy version.**

Preheat the oven to 170°C.

Trim and wash the baby carrots, but don't peel them (they look super-cute whole or halved lengthways). Place the carrots on a greased baking tray. Drizzle over the maple syrup, dot with 2 tablespoons of the coconut oil and season to taste with chilli flakes, salt and pepper. (I find it easiest to get my hands in there and make sure everything is coated evenly.) Bake for 20 minutes (they should still have a little bit of crunch).

Meanwhile, slice each chicken breast in half lengthways. Break the eggs into a shallow bowl, whisk and set aside. In another shallow bowl combine the almond meal, lemon zest and parsley, stirring well. Now for the fun stuff! Dip one chicken fillet into the egg mix and then roll it in the almond meal mixture until it is thickly coated. Repeat with the remaining chicken pieces.

Heat the remaining coconut oil in a large frying pan over a medium heat. Place the chicken fillets in the pan and cook for 2–3 minutes on each side or until cooked through and golden brown (you may need to cook them in two batches if you have a smallish pan). Place two fillets on each plate with the sweet baby carrots and some sliced avocado. Finish with a drizzle of olive oil, a squeeze of lemon and a twist of freshly ground black pepper. Scrumbo!

SERVES 4

# CHICKEN BURGERS IN LETTUCE CUPS

3 tablespoons coconut oil
1 brown onion, diced
1 carrot, grated
1 zucchini, grated
2 stalks celery, diced
500 g chicken mince
1 teaspoon chilli flakes
35 g (⅓ cup) almond meal
2 eggs, lightly beaten
salt
freshly ground black pepper
6 butter lettuce cups
2 large tomatoes, sliced
  into rounds
2 avocados, sliced lengthways
olive oil, to serve
sesame seeds, to serve
extra chilli flakes, optional

## TIP

These burgers make yummy leftovers: serve them with a quinoa salad (see page 98) or a farmers market salad (see page 120), or pop them in a gluten-free wrap for lunch.

**I love using lettuce cups to hold these burgers, but there's nothing stopping you from having yours with flat bread or gluten-free bread. I don't use iceberg because it has less flavour (and fewer nutrients) than other varieties, but go with whatever floats your boat.**

Melt 2 tablespoons of the coconut oil in a frying pan over a medium heat. Sauté the onion, carrot, zucchini and celery for 2–3 minutes or until the vegetables are softened and the onion is golden. Transfer them to a mixing bowl and allow them to cool. Add the chicken mince, chilli flakes, 2 tablespoons of the almond meal, eggs and season to taste. Mix well, divide into 6 portions, and shape each into a pattie. Transfer to a plate, cover and refrigerate for 2–3 hours.

When the patties are firm, remove from the fridge. Place the remaining 2 tablespoons of almond meal in a shallow bowl. Roll each pattie in the almond meal, coating it evenly.

Heat the remaining coconut oil in a large frying pan over a medium heat. Place 3 patties in the pan and cook them for about 5 minutes on each side, or until golden and cooked through. Repeat with the remaining patties.

To serve, place 3 lettuce cups on each plate. Line each cup with equal portions of the tomato rounds and avocado slices, then pop a pattie on top, drizzle with olive oil and sprinkle with sesame seeds and chilli flakes (if using). And you don't even need a knife and fork!

SERVES 2

# CRISPY CHICKEN THIGHS WITH VEGGIE MIX-UP

**My mate Bridget made this dish for me one night and I loved it so much I asked if I could use it in the book. (She actually calls the veggie part 'the veggie mess', which makes me laugh!) So with her blessing, here it is.**

Heat 2 tablespoons of the coconut oil in a frying pan over a medium heat. Sauté the sweet potato for 5–7 minutes or until soft. Add the spinach, cherry toms and zucchini. Season to taste with salt, pepper and chilli flakes and cook for 4–5 minutes or until the zucchini has softened. Cover and keep warm.

Heat the remaining 2 tablespoons of coconut oil in another frying pan over a medium heat and add the chicken. The trick to making them super crispy is to cook them until golden on one side then move them about so the other sides are cooked. This should take 2–3 minutes depending on how thinly you've sliced your fillets.

To serve, divide your 'veggie mess' between two plates and top with golden chicken fillets and diced avocado. Drizzle over olive oil and sprinkle with fresh coriander leaves.

SERVES 2

80 ml (⅓ cup) coconut oil
1 sweet potato, cut into 5 cm cubes
160 g (4 cups) chopped spinach
250 g (2 cups) cherry tomatoes, halved
1 zucchini, sliced
salt
freshly ground black pepper
chilli flakes
6 chicken thigh fillets, sliced into thin strips
1 large avocado, diced
olive oil, to serve
coriander leaves, to serve

# ROAST CHICKEN WITH QUINOA, PISTACHIO AND CRANBERRY STUFFING

1 cup quinoa, rinsed

80 ml (⅓ cup) coconut oil

1 brown onion, finely diced

1 pear, cored, finely diced

70 g (½ cup) chopped pistachios

60 g (½ cup) dried cranberries

1 × 1.5 kg chicken

1 lemon, quartered

6 thyme sprigs

2 large carrots, roughly chopped

2 stalks celery, roughly chopped

1 red onion, cut into chunks

salt

freshly ground black pepper

## TIPS

Feel free to change the herbs and berries in the stuffing to reflect the season. I like to eat the trivet vegetables because they're lovely and sweet and caramelised, but you can serve the chicken with any salad or veggie accompaniment.

**Cooking up a big roast might seem a bit daunting, but it's really not that hard. I'm no professional in the kitchen, that's for sure, but I've still done lots of Christmas turkeys.**

Preheat the oven to 220°C. Place the quinoa in a saucepan with 2 cups of water, cover and bring to the boil. Reduce the heat and simmer for 10 minutes until the quinoa is cooked (it triples in size and sprouts little 'tails').

Heat 2 tablespoons of the coconut oil in a frying pan over a medium heat. Sauté the onion for 2 minutes or until translucent. Add the pear and cook until it begins to soften (about 4–6 minutes). Remove from the heat.

In a large bowl place the pistachios, cranberries and cooked quinoa. Fold through the onion and pear combo and mix well. Spoon the mixture into the chicken cavity, pressing firmly. Finally, pop the four lemon quarters and thyme sprigs in.

Place the carrots, celery and red onion in the baking dish (this will become your 'trivet', which elevates the chicken so it cooks evenly). Pop the stuffed chicken on top. Rub the remaining 2 tablespoons of coconut oil into the chicken skin, and give it a generous seasoning with salt and pepper (this will help it to become crispy). Reduce the oven temperate to 200°C and roast for 1–1¼ hours or until the skin is golden and the juices run clear when you pierce the thigh with a knife point. (If the juices are pink, roast for another 10 minutes.)

Remove the chicken from the oven and allow it to rest for 10 minutes before carving. Serve with the trivet vegetables (or a side of your choosing) and some stuffing, and I promise you everyone will be coming back for seconds!

SERVES 6

# LAMB CUTLETS WITH CAULIFLOWER RICE AND CHILLI SAUCE

**Cauliflower rice may sound weird, but when cooked and processed, cauliflower gives you the same consistency and texture as rice without having to eat grains, and you can tweak the flavours as much as you like.**

Process the cauliflower in a food processor until it resembles rice. Place the cauliflower and stock in a large saucepan over a medium heat and bring to the boil. Reduce heat and simmer, uncovered, for 20 minutes. Remove from the heat and allow to cool slightly (this prevents the olive oil from oxidising). Stir through the olive oil and lemon juice, season to taste, cover and keep warm.

Combine the tomatoes, garlic, onion, chillies, salt and pepper in another saucepan. Place over a medium heat and bring to the boil. Reduce heat and simmer for 5–7 minutes, or until this delish combo thickens.

Meanwhile, heat the coconut oil in a frying pan over a medium heat. Cook the cutlets for 2–3 minutes on each side, or until golden in colour. Serve the cutlets with the chilli–tomato sauce and cauliflower rice, season to taste and enjoy this clean, nourishing meal!

SERVES 2–3

400 g (4 cups) cauliflower florets
500 ml (2 cups) stock, chicken or veggie
2 tablespoons olive oil
juice of ½ lemon
salt
freshly ground black pepper
2 × 400 g cans chopped tomatoes
4 garlic cloves, finely diced
1 brown onion, finely diced
2 red chillies, finely diced
2 tablespoons coconut oil
6 × 75 g lamb cutlets

TIP

If you're not into meat, simply make the cauliflower rice and serve it with a veggie curry (page 119), some baked mushies (page 53), or your favourite veggie dish.

# SPICY ROO STEAKS WITH MANGO AND AVOCADO SALSA

**Kangaroo meat is super healthy (low in fat, high in iron and protein) and easy on the environment, so it gets the thumbs-up from me. But if eating meat isn't your thing, the salsa goes with pretty much anything: try it with a green salad, a fluffy batch of quinoa or just eat it by itself. Yum!**

Combine the mango, avocado, cherry tomatoes, onion, chilli and coriander in a large bowl. Dress with the lemon juice and olive oil, season to taste, mix well and set aside.

Season both sides of the roo fillets with paprika, salt and pepper. Heat the coconut oil in a heavy-based frying pan over a medium heat. Cook the fillets for 3–4 minutes on each side, then allow to rest for 5 minutes.

To serve, mound some salsa on each plate, and place a sliced kanga fillet beside it. Top the salsa with half the lime juice and zest and a few sprigs of fresh coriander. Job done!

SERVES 2

2 mangoes, diced
2 avocados, diced
120 g (1 cup) cherry
   tomatoes, halved
1 small red onion, diced
1 small red chilli, finely
   chopped
60 g (2 cups) coriander
   leaves, roughly chopped
juice of 1 lemon
1–2 tablespoons olive oil
salt
freshly ground black pepper
2 × 150 g kangaroo fillets
1 teaspoon paprika
2 tablespoons coconut oil
zest and juice of 1 lime
coriander sprigs, to serve

# PERFECT STEAKS WITH GREEN FAIRY TREE SALAD

180 g (2 cups) broccoli
  florets
1 Granny Smith apple, peeled
  and grated
3 tablespoons raisins
60 g (½ cup) walnuts, chopped
3 tablespoons olive oil
1 tablespoon balsamic
  vinegar
salt
freshly ground black pepper
2 tablespoons coconut oil
2 × 180–200 g beef steaks

**Many people ask me how to cook the perfect steak, so here is my favourite way to cook lovely medium—rare steaks. As for the salad, one of the most amazing beings I know (I call her my surrogate mum, but she prefers the term 'soul sister') would add a little broccoli to my dinner each night, explaining that if I ate the 'green fairy trees' the magic would pass onto me. Naturally I happily gobbled up my magical 'fairy trees'! Thanks, Linda! You made me one healthy little kiddlet!**

Pour 2 cups of water into a saucepan with a steamer and bring to the boil over a medium–high heat. Place the broccoli florets in the steamer and cook for 3–4 minutes, or until the broccoli has softened but still has a bit of crunch. (It should look nice and bright.) Set aside to cool.

Combine the broccoli, apple, raisins and walnuts in a large bowl. Whisk the olive oil and balsamic vinegar in a jug and season to taste. Pour over the broccoli salad, toss and set aside.

Heat the coconut oil in a frying pan over a medium heat. Cook the steaks in the pan for 3–4 minutes on one side, then turn over and cook for a further 2 minutes. Remove from the heat and allow to rest for 4–5 minutes.

Divide your fairy tree salad between two plates and top with the steak. (I always pour the pan juices over the meat for added flavour.) Season to taste with freshly ground black pepper and a good-quality salt (Himalayan or Murray River pink salt).

SERVES 2

# PALEO SHEPHERD'S PIE

**This is a pretty hearty meal, yet with the cauliflower topping it's a very low carbohydrate meal. I love making this for dinner after I've done a big workout and want to get loads of protein to my muscles.**

Preheat the oven to 180°C.

Heat the coconut oil in a large frying pan and sauté the onion for 2 minutes or until translucent. Add the carrot, celery and spices and cook for another minute. Season to taste, then add the beef and cook for 1–2 minutes or until slightly browned. Pour in the chicken stock and simmer for 5–10 minutes or until reduced to a thick, stewy consistency.

Meanwhile, place the cauliflower and olive oil in your food processor, season and blitz until the cauliflower is crumbly (it looks a bit like rice).

Pour the beef mixture into the base of a 33 × 23 cm baking dish. Top with the cauliflower mash and bake for 30 minutes. Remove it from the oven, allow it to cool, then *dig in*!

SERVES 6

2 tablespoons coconut oil
1 brown onion, diced
2 carrots, grated
2 stalks celery, finely
  chopped
½ teaspoon paprika
½ teaspoon ground cumin
salt
freshly ground black pepper
500 g minced beef
250 ml (1 cup) chicken stock
600 g (6 cups) cauliflower
  florets
2 tablespoons olive oil

# MEXICAN CHILLI BEEF WITH GUACAMOLE AND SWEET POTATO

**I'm a sucker for chilli — somehow it seems to sneak its way into just about everything I make (even some of my smoothies!). But chillies are so good for me that I'm happy to overload on them. They speed up your metabolic rate (good for weight control), promote heart health and are full of antioxidants (which are great for skin health). This is my take on an old classic. Enjoy!**

Heat the coconut oil in a deep frying pan or heavy-based saucepan over a medium heat and sauté the brown onion for 2 minutes or until translucent. Add the garlic and cook for 30 seconds (it becomes translucent really quickly). Add the mince and cook for 2–3 minutes, breaking it up with a wooden spoon so it cooks evenly. Stir in the tomatoes, fresh chillies, crushed cumin seeds and 1 teaspoon of the paprika and bring to a simmer. Add the cherry tomatoes and lime (in two halves), season to taste and let it simmer away for 10–12 minutes.

Meanwhile, wash your sweet spuds and slice them thinly into rounds with a mandolin or a very sharp knife (you can slice them in half again to make half moons if you like).

Place the avocado in a large mixing bowl and mash it roughly with the back of a fork. Add the cumin, lime juice and zest (reserving a pinch for garnish), red onion, coriander, diced tomato, chilli, olive oil and and remaining teaspoon of paprika and give it a really good mash. Season to taste and pop it in a pretty bowl. Sprinkle with pumpkin seeds, a little more paprika and the reserved smidge of lime zest and finish with a drizzle of olive oil.

When ready to serve, remove the lime halves from the chilli. Now there are two ways to serve this clean, lean meal: you can place the chilli beef, avocado magicness and spuddy dippers in the centre of your table and dig in, or you can serve individual portions of the chilli beef, guacamole and dippers on serving plates and enjoy!

SERVES 4

2 tablespoons coconut oil
1 brown onion, finely diced
3 garlic cloves, finely diced
500 g beef mince
2 × 400 g cans diced tomatoes
2 red chillies, finely chopped
1 teaspoon cumin seeds, crushed
2 teaspoons paprika
250 g (2 cups) cherry tomatoes, halved
1 lime, halved
salt
freshly ground black pepper
2 sweet potatoes

## GUACAMOLE

4 large avocados, diced
½ teaspoon ground cumin
zest and juice of 1 lime
½ red onion, finely diced
30 g (1 cup) coriander leaves, finely chopped
1 tomato, diced
1 red chilli, finely chopped
2 tablespoons olive oil
1 teaspoon pumpkin seeds, to serve
extra paprika, to serve
extra olive oil, to serve

# ROO BOLOGNESE WITH RAW ZUCCHINI SPAGHETTI

**This is known as 'rooghetti' at my house. Kangaroo meat is super lean and full of nutrients, but like all game meats, it can have a strong taste. A bolognese sauce is an ideal way to tame flavour, plus the addition of lime is a brilliant tweak that really lifts the flavour (thanks for the tip, Kane!).**

Heat the coconut oil in a deep frying pan over a medium heat. Sauté the onion until translucent (about 2–3 minutes) then add the garlic and cook a further minute. Add the kangaroo mince, breaking up any lumps with a wooden spoon so it cooks evenly. Cook for 2–3 minutes, or until the meat begins to brown. Add the tomatoes, tomato paste, carrot, dried herbs, lime juice and both halves of the squeezed lime (keep them as halves so they're easy to remove later). Add 3 cups of water, season to taste and bring to the boil. Reduce heat to the lowest setting, stir, cover and cook for 2 hours.

Using a spiral veggie slicer or pawpaw grater, grate 1 zucchini into each bowl to make your raw pasta. Spoon over the hot bolognese sauce and enjoy your rooghetti!

SERVES 4

2 tablespoons coconut oil
1 large brown onion, finely diced
2 garlic cloves, finely diced
600 g kangaroo mince
1 × 400 g can tomatoes
1 tablespoon tomato paste
2 carrots, grated
1 teaspoon dried oregano
½ teaspoon dried thyme
juice of 1 lime
salt
freshly ground black pepper
4 zucchini, grated

TIP

If you don't have a spiral veggie slicer (see page 20), just buy a green pawpaw grater at any Asian grocery store; they cost about $3 and make the best zucchini pasta strips.

You've probably guessed by now that I'm a sweet tooth, so you'll know that these recipes are all going to be delicious as well as good for you. But sweet food is not something you're supposed to have for every single meal — that's why I call it a 'treat'. You see, our bodies aren't designed to cope with the massive amounts of sugar in our Western diet, and the long-term health effects are pretty shocking. The term sugar refers to simple carbohydrates including sucrose (table sugar), fructose (fruit sugar) and lactose (milk sugar). These guys are quickly converted to glucose when they enter our bodies, giving us an immediate energy hit. The problem is, if we don't use that glucose, it will not only cause an insulin spike (where a stack of insulin is released to mop up the glucose), but any left over will get stored as fat. When the insulin finishes its job, usually about 90 minutes or so after eating, we get a sudden drop in glucose, which in turn triggers our hunger hormones (and also makes us feel a bit flat and lacking in energy). So even though we really don't *need* to eat any more food, our body craves it! You can see how this can become a vicious circle, leading to weight issues and, over the long term, can become a precursor for obesity, diabetes and heart disease.

But there are natural sweeteners that cause less of a blood sugar spike (and crash) than sucrose and also contain heaps of nutrients. These include coconut nectar, coconut sugar, medjool dates, raw honey, maple syrup and agave. I use them a lot for making treats, but always in moderation. I also use another natural sweetener: stevia (extracted from the *Stevia rebaudiana* plant), which doesn't cause insulin spikes at all, though it can have a bitter aftertaste if you use too much. There are so many options for you to try, so have a play and see what works best for you.

# SWEET TREATS

# RAW ENERGY SUPERFOOD BALLS

155 g (1 cup) almonds
100 g (1 cup) walnuts
360 g (2 cups) medjool
  dates, pitted
2 tablespoons LSA
2 tablespoons chia seeds
3 tablespoons coconut oil,
  melted
3 tablespoons cacao powder
½ teaspoon cinnamon
60 g (½ cup) goji berries

## COATING

3 tablespoons chia seeds
3 tablespoons desiccated
  coconut
3 tablespoons chopped
  almonds
3 tablespoons goji berries,
  chopped

**These are the perfect snack, dessert or even pressie. My awesomely inspiring mate Faustina, who tested this recipe for me, asked if the caffeine in them would keep her awake. The answer is no, since there's only a small amount of cacao and it has very little caffeine compared to tea or coffee anyway. Also, raw cacao is a natural source of the mineral magnesium which actually helps to calm you down and relax you before you sleep. So this is the perfect any-time snack!**

Place all the ingredients in a food processor and whizz for 30 seconds or more, depending on the strength of your processor. If the mixture seems too thick to easily form into balls, add ¼ cup water and whizz again.

Combine the chia seeds, coconut, almonds and goji berries in a large bowl and give them a good mix-up.

Roll teaspoons of the mixture into little balls using your hands. Roll the balls in your topping mix to coat and place half in the fridge for munching over the next few days, and the rest in a plastic container in the freezer for another time.

MAKES 18–24

## TIP

'LSA' is ground linseed, sunflower seeds and almonds — a major nutrient hit!

# GRAIN-FREE BLUEBERRY AND COCONUT MUFFINS

**These yummy muffins are high in protein to give you sustained energy without the sugar rush and crash you get from highly processed grains and sucrose. I've put them here as a dessert, but they are a perfect brekkie or snack to help keep you on the 20/20 Diet path.**

Preheat the oven to 180°C. Line 2 × 6-hole or 1 × 12-hole muffin trays with paper.

Combine the almond meal and baking powder in a large bowl and mix well. Add the eggs, coconut oil, almond milk, cinnamon, vanilla seeds, maple syrup and mix thoroughly until lump-free. (You'll have to work pretty quickly so the coconut oil doesn't go solid.) Gently fold through the shredded coconut and blueberries.

Spoon the mixture into the paper-lined muffin tray. Sprinkle with a few shards of coconut and bake for 20–30 minutes or until golden and a skewer inserted into the centre of a muffin comes out clean. Allow the muffins to cool slightly then enjoy! (I love to cut one in half while it's still warm and spread almond butter inside!)

MAKES 12 LARGE MUFFINS

300 g (3 cups) almond meal
2 teaspoons gluten-free baking powder
4 eggs, lightly beaten
125 ml (½ cup) coconut oil, melted
80 ml (⅓ cup) almond milk
1 teaspoon ground cinnamon
1 vanilla pod, split and scraped
80 ml (⅓ cup) maple syrup
60 g (1 cup) shredded coconut
300 g (2 cups) blueberries, fresh or frozen
**extra shredded coconut, to garnish**

## TIPS

If you don't have a vanilla pod handy, use ½ teaspoon of powdered pure vanilla. Also feel free to substitute raw honey, coconut nectar or brown rice syrup for the maple syrup.

# ZUCCHINI CHOC-CHIP MINI-MUFFINS

coconut oil, for greasing

2 medium zucchini, grated

4 eggs, lightly beaten

125 ml (½ cup) coconut oil, melted

80 ml (⅓ cup) maple syrup

60 g (½ cup) cacao powder

2 heaped tablespoons coconut flour

50 g (½ cup) almond meal

60 g (½ cup) cacao nibs

1 vanilla pod, split and scraped

1 teaspoon ground cinnamon

½ teaspoon ground nutmeg

1 teaspoon gluten-free baking powder

pinch pink salt

## TIP

Mini-muffin pans usually come in 12s or 24s. If you don't have one, simply use a regular 6- or 12-hole muffin pan, or bake the mixture in a loaf tin.

**These little beauties make the perfect mid-morning snack and are a delicious, nourishing alternative to a traditional chocolate cake with its heavy mix of dairy, wheat flour and sugar.**

Preheat the oven to 180°C. Grease your muffin tray (or loaf tin) with a little coconut oil.

Place the grated zucchini in a mesh sieve and press with your hands to remove excess liquid. Drain on paper towel (or clean tea towel) and twist to remove the last of the water.

Combine all of the ingredients in a large mixing bowl and mix thoroughly. (The batter should have a nice even consistency, and should smell and look quite chocolatey.) Spoon the batter into each hole of the mini-muffin tray to about two-thirds full. Cook for 15–20 minutes, or until a skewer inserted into a centre muffin comes out clean. (Cook larger muffins for 20–25 minutes, and a loaf for 25–30 minutes.)

Remove from the oven and allow to cool. (Or, if you're like me, wait about 5 minutes, cut a slice, and top it with almond butter, coconut nectar and cinnamon!)

MAKES 36 MINI-MUFFINS OR 12 REGULAR MUFFINS

# BANANA AND PECAN MUFFINS

These sweet treats are as close to guilt-free as you can get because the only thing we are using to sweeten this recipe is bananas — *so* natural!

Preheat the oven to 180°C. Line 2 × 6-hole or 1 × 12-hole muffin trays with paper patty cases.

In a large mixing bowl combine all the ingredients and mix thoroughly, ensuring all lumps are smoothed out. Spoon into the muffin liners and bake for 20 minutes (or until a skewer comes out clean when inserted into the centre of one of the muffins).

Enjoy warm, spread with almond butter and coconut nectar.

MAKES 12

3 large bananas, mashed
4 eggs, lightly beaten
1 vanilla pod, split and scraped
250 ml (1 cup) coconut cream
50 g (½ cup) almond meal
60 g (½ cup) coconut flour
½ teaspoon ground cinnamon
¼ teaspoon ground nutmeg
30 g (¼ cup) finely chopped pecans
3 tablespoons coconut oil, melted

# CHOCOLATE MACAROONS

**This recipe is so easy, and is especially fun to make with kids.**

Preheat the oven to 160°C.

Place all ingredients in a food processor and blend (or you could mix by hand). Use dampened hands to form teaspoon-sized balls of the mixture and place them on a lined baking tray. Press them down slightly (so they don't roll around) and bake them for 15 minutes. Allow to cool, then enjoy with your fellow cooks!

MAKES ABOUT 24

## TIPS

These are delicious raw, too, but if you want some crunch, cook them as described above. Also feel free to tweak them by adding goji berries or even chilli (as I've been known to do!).

135 g (1½ cups) desiccated coconut
100 g (1 cup) almond meal
3 tablespoons coconut oil, melted
60 g (½ cup) cacao powder
125 ml (½ cup) coconut nectar
pinch pink salt

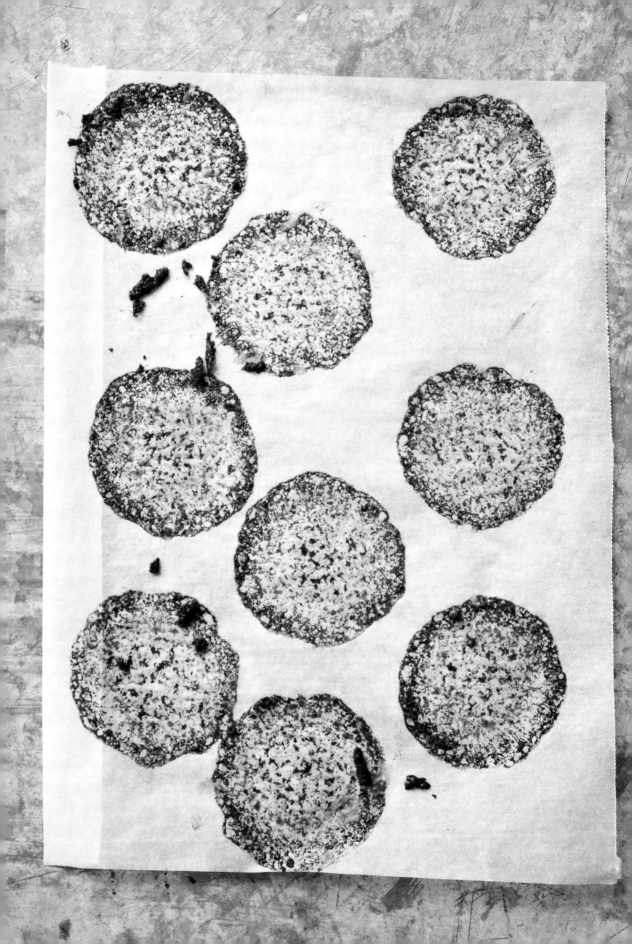

# APPLE-CINNAMON COOKIES

**These little snacks are all-round winners. The fruit, nuts and oats are a great source of fibre, the cinnamon is a potent antioxidant and the apple pectin and oats are linked to lowering cholesterol. (I make these for my dad and call them his 'cholesterol-lowering cookies'!)**

Preheat the oven to 180°C. Line a tray with baking paper and place ½ cup of the oats in a small bowl, ready for rolling.

Combine the mashed banana, remaining 2 cups of oats, walnuts, raisins, grated apple, maple syrup, vanilla, coconut oil, cinnamon and salt in a large bowl. Mix well using your hands (it helps to keep the coconut oil soft). Then shape into balls, roll them in the oats and place on the baking tray, flattening just a touch with your hands.

Reduce the oven temperature to 160°C and bake these little babies for 25–30 minutes, or until golden brown. Now you can either let them cool, or make a simple and delicious dessert. Place 2 in a little bowl and top with a scoop of coconut ice cream or dollop of yoghurt, a drizzle of maple syrup and a dash of cinnamon. Try it!

## MAKES 12 BIG COOKIES

250 g (2 ½ cups) rolled oats
1 banana, mashed
60 g (½ cup) roughly chopped walnuts
80 g (½ cup) raisins or sultanas
150 g (1 cup) grated apple
2 tablespoons maple syrup
1 vanilla pod, split and scraped or ½ teaspoon powdered vanilla
3 tablespoons coconut oil, melted
½ teaspoon ground cinnamon
pinch pink salt

## TIPS

I love using granny smith apples for these cookies. Also, if you can't tolerate oats, this works fine with quinoa flakes.

# RAW VANILLA MACAROON BALLS

**These are simply *heaven*! I'm giving you the vanilla recipe but you can whip up your own version with cacao or goji berries.**

Combine all the ingredients in a large bowl and mix thoroughly. If the mixture is too crumbly, add a little more coconut oil and another tablespoon of maple syrup. Shape into little balls (it's easier with damp hands), arrange them on a tray and whack them in the freezer for about 20 minutes to set. Store in an airtight container in the fridge and share them with your mates.

MAKES ABOUT 20

125 ml (½ cup) coconut oil, melted
50 g (½ cup) almond meal
3 tablespoons maple syrup
90 g (1 cup) desiccated coconut
1 vanilla pod, split and scraped
pinch pink salt

# ANZACS WITH A TWIST

**People with gluten or dairy intolerance don't have to miss out on Anzac cookies with these little treaties. I've even added an extra Aussie twist with macadamia nuts.**

Preheat the oven to 160°C. Line a large tray with baking paper.

Combine the oats, coconut, macadamia nuts and bananas in a large bowl. Add the melted coconut oil, maple syrup and vanilla and mix well. Roll tablespoons of mixture into balls, place on the tray and flatten gently. (Sometimes I use heart cutters — I know, hopeless romantic!)

Reduce the oven temperature to 140°C and bake for 10–15 minutes or until golden brown. Allow to cool if you want some crunch, but if you're like me, sneak one while they're still hot!

MAKES ABOUT 20

150 g (1½ cups) rolled oats
30 g (½ cup) shredded coconut
80 g (½ cup) macadamia
  nuts, roughly chopped
2 large bananas, mashed
125 ml (½ cup) coconut oil,
  melted
125 ml (½ cup) maple syrup
½ vanilla pod, split and scraped
pinch pink salt

## TIPS

One third of people who are gluten-intolerant also react to oats, so if you're not sure, maybe try these out when you're at home and don't have to go out anywhere. (That's what I do!) Feel free to use desiccated coconut and ¼ teaspoon of pure vanilla powder if you're out of shredded coconut and vanilla pods.

# VEGAN SWEET POTATO BROWNIES

2 large sweet potatoes,
  cubed
360 g (2 cups) medjool
  dates, pitted
60 g (½ cup) roughly
  chopped walnuts
100 g (1 cup) almond meal
40 g (⅓ cup) cacao powder
60 g (½ cup) goji berries
tiny pinch chilli flakes
80 ml (⅓ cup) maple syrup
pinch salt

**These guys are loaded with nutrients. They have nuts for protein, chewy goji berries for antioxidants and a chilli kick to boost your metabolism!**

Preheat the oven to 180°C. Line the base and sides of a square cake tin with baking paper.

Place the sweet potato in a saucepan of boiling water and cook until soft (15–20 minutes). Drain, cool slightly and transfer to your food processor along with the dates. Blend until super smooth then transfer to a large bowl. Add the remaining ingredients and give it a really good mix-up.

Spoon the mixture evenly into the cake tin and bake for 20 minutes. Allow to cool for 10 minutes, slice and serve.

MAKES ABOUT 12 PIECES

# QUINOA BANANA BREAD

**A delicious gluten-free, dairy-free banana bread!**

Preheat the oven to 180°C. Grease a loaf tin with coconut oil and set aside.

Place the quinoa flour, quinoa flakes, baking powder, spices and salt in a bowl and mix thoroughly.

In a smaller bowl, mash your narnies then stir in the eggs, melted coconut oil and maple syrup.

Make a well in the centre of your dry ingredients and pour in the banana mixture. Mix well, using a wooden spoon to smooth out any lumpy bits. (You can use an electric cake mixer if you like, but there's something soothing about using the old school hands-on way, plus I reckon whatever you cook will taste better!)

Pour the batter into your loaf tin and bake for 20–25 minutes (insert a skewer to check that it's cooked through — if it comes out clean, it is). Allow to cool and share it with someone you love, even if that someone is you!

SERVES 8

coconut oil, for greasing
200 g (1 cup) quinoa flour
60 g (½ cup) quinoa flakes
2 teaspoons gluten-free baking powder
½ teaspoon ground cinnamon
¼ teaspoon ground nutmeg
pinch salt
2 large super-ripe bananas
2 large eggs, lightly beaten
3 tablespoons coconut oil, melted
3 tablespoons maple syrup

# EASY-PEASY MOUSSE

**This recipe has been in my cooking repertoire for a while now and everyone loves it. No-one ever guesses this is made with avocado!**

Pop your avocado, dates, bananas, cacao powder, cinnamon and salt in your processor and blend until it's smooth and silky (about 40–50 seconds). Then serve in bowls and top with fresh mint. Delishimo!

SERVES 4

2 large avocados
6 medjool dates, pitted
2 frozen bananas
3 tablespoons cacao powder
½ teaspoon ground cinnamon
**pinch pink salt**
**mint sprigs, to serve**

TIP
If you don't like dates, substitute ¼ cup of raw honey, maple syrup or coconut nectar — whatever floats your boat.

# TASHI'S RAW ROSE AND RASPBERRY TART

10 medjool dates, pitted
1 tablespoon coconut oil
30 g (½ cup) linseed meal
80 g (½ cup) chia seeds
70 g (1 cup) shredded
   coconut
125 g (1 cup) raspberries,
   to serve
rose petals, to serve

## CREAM FILLING

250 g (1¾ cups) cashews,
   soaked (4–6 hours) and
   rinsed
80 ml (⅓ cup) coconut oil,
   melted
85 ml (⅓ cup) coconut nectar
   or raw honey
125 g (1 cup) raspberries,
   fresh or frozen
¼ teaspoon rosewater
   essence
3 tablespoons 100% pure
   pomegranate juice

**This mind-blowingly amazing raw tart comes from an equally amazing friend of mine. Thank you, Tashi! Try serving it with coconut ice cream.**

Blend the dates and coconut oil in a food processor. Add the linseed meal, chia seeds and shredded coconut and process until the mixture has a biscuity consistency. Press the mixture into the base and sides of a pie dish or loose-bottomed tart tin. Refrigerate for at least 6 hours (ideally overnight).

To make the cream filling, blend the cashews, coconut oil and coconut nectar in a high-powered food processor. Add the raspberries, rosewater essence and pomegranate juice and blend until very smooth. If your mixture needs a little more liquid, just top it up with a smidgen of pomegranate juice. Pour over the now-firm biscuity base and refrigerate for another 8 hours.

Slice and serve with fresh berries and a pinch of rose petals. A beautiful dessert for a special occasion!

## SERVES 12

## TIPS

Rosewater essence is a more concentrated form of rosewater. If you only have rosewater, use 1½ teaspoons. And if you can't find edible rose petals, use some of the petals from rose tea. This recipe needs to be started the night before.

# EPIC RAW BANOFFEE PIE

**This is a cleaner and much healthier version of the famous English pie traditionally made with pastry, banana, cream and toffee.**

Blitz the almonds and pecans into a paste using a sturdy food processor. Add the desiccated coconut, dates, almond butter and coconut oil and process until the mixture is biscuity. Press the mixture into the base and sides of a pie dish or loose-bottomed tart tin (it helps if you have damp hands). Pop in the freezer for 2 hours to set.

To prepare the filling, place the cashews in your blender and process until creamy. Add the bananas, coconut water, coconut oil and medjool dates and again process until creamy (about 60 seconds). When the pie base is firm, pour the banana mixture on top and return to the freezer for 2 hours.

To make the toffee, combine the dates (removed from the soaking water), almond butter, coconut oil, maple syrup, vanilla seeds and salt in your food processor. Blend on the highest speed until super smooth (add the almond milk if you prefer it a bit runnier). Pour into a serving jug.

When the pie filling is set, remove from the freezer. Slice the remaining banana and arrange the discs neatly over the top of the cake. Drizzle over the toffee, sprinkle with cinnamon and enjoy your delicious, healthy masterpiece!

## SERVES 12

## TIP

You'll need to start this the night before, by soaking the almonds, pecans and cashews overnight.

## CRUST

80 g (½ cup) almonds, soaked and rinsed
60 g (½ cup) pecans, soaked and rinsed
45 g (½ cup) desiccated coconut
180 g (1 cup) medjool dates, pitted
2 tablespoons almond butter
2 tablespoons coconut oil

## CREAM

150 g (1 cup) cashews, soaked and rinsed
2 bananas
60 ml (¼ cup) coconut water
2 tablespoons coconut oil
4 medjool dates, pitted

## TOFFEE

180 g (1 cup) medjool dates, pitted and soaked in 2 cups boiled water
125 g (½ cup) almond butter
125 ml (½ cup) coconut oil, melted
3 tablespoons maple syrup
½ vanilla pod, split and scraped
pinch salt
3 tablespoons almond milk, optional

## TO SERVE

1 banana
ground cinnamon

# RAW LIME AND AVOCADO PIE

## CRUST

80 g (½ cup) almonds, soaked and rinsed

60 g (½ cup) pecans, soaked and rinsed

180 g (1 cup) medjool dates, pitted

2 tablespoons almond butter

60 g (¾ cup) desiccated coconut

185 ml (¾ cup) coconut oil, melted

## FILLING

2 large avocados

125 ml (½ cup) maple syrup

juice and zest of 2 limes

1 vanilla pod, split and scraped

60 g (½ cup) shredded coconut, to serve

## TIPS

Soaking the almonds and pecans simply enables your body to process their nutrients more quickly. If you don't have a vanilla pod, use ½ teaspoon pure vanilla powder instead. Also, feel free to substitute a sweetener of your choice for the maple syrup. The best time to make this is probably first thing in the morning, so that it will be ready by dinnertime.

**This is one of those sweet treats that will blow people away, especially when they learn that it's raw and mostly made from avocado! I honestly believe it was this recipe that got me hooked on raw food.**

Blitz the almonds and pecans in a good food processor. Add the dates, almond butter, ½ cup of the desiccated coconut and ¼ cup of the coconut oil and blitz again. Spoon this crumbly mixture into a pie dish or loose-bottomed tart tin and press it evenly into the base and sides (it helps to have damp hands). Pop the dish in the freezer for 2 hours to set.

Process the avocados, maple syrup, lime juice, ½ the lime zest, vanilla seeds, remaining ½ cup of coconut oil and ¼ cup of desiccated coconut in a blender until smooth.

When the crust is firm, remove the pie dish from the freezer. Spoon over the avocado mixture and place in the fridge to set for about 8 hours.

When set, sprinkle with shredded coconut and the remaining lime zest.

SERVES 12

# SWEET POTATO PIE

**This recipe came to me in a dream — seriously! At first I didn't think it would work because I'm used to sweet spuds in savoury dishes, but after a few trials I discovered it really does!**

Preheat the oven to 180°C. Grease a pie dish with a little coconut oil.

Process the almonds, dates, coconut, almond butter and coconut oil until biscuity. Dampen your hands and press the mixture evenly into the base and sides of the pie dish. Pop in the freezer for 2 hours to set.

Meanwhile, place the sweet potato on a baking tray. Drizzle over ½ cup of the coconut oil and dust with a good shake of cinnamon (do it from high up so it coats the potato evenly). Cook for 20–30 minutes or until soft. Remove from the oven and allow to cool. Place the sweet potato in your food processor along with the dates, maple syrup, cinnamon, nutmeg, salt and remaining ¼ cup of coconut oil. Process until you have a lovely smooth texture (do yourself a favour and taste the raw mixture, it is amazing).

Remove the pie base from the freezer and spoon over the filling. Return the pie to the freezer for 2 hours. When set, decorate with pecans and enjoy this wonderful flavour bomb!

SERVES 12

coconut oil, for greasing

## CRUST
- 155 g (1 cup) almonds, soaked and rinsed
- 180 g (1 cup) medjool dates, pitted
- 3 tablespoons desiccated coconut
- 2 tablespoons almond butter
- 125 ml (½ cup) coconut oil, melted

## FILLING
- 2 large sweet potatoes, cut into 5 cm cubes
- 185 ml (¾ cup) coconut oil, melted
- good shake of ground cinnamon
- 8 medjool dates, pitted
- 2 tablespoons maple syrup
- ½ teaspoon ground cinnamon
- ¼ teaspoon ground nutmeg
- pinch salt
- 60 g (½ cup) pecans, to garnish

# PUMPKIN AND PECAN PIE

**This yummy Americana-style recipe (pumpkin pie and pecan pie are both American classics) is a brilliant source of healthy spices, plus you're getting protein, nutrients and fibre from the nuts, fruit and pumpkin. A dessert that nurtures — cool!**

Preheat the oven to 180°C.

Place the almonds, pecans, raisins and dates in a food processor and blend. Add the melted coconut oil, desiccated coconut and maple syrup and blend until the mixture is thick and biscuity. Press the mixture into the base and sides of a pie dish or loose-bottomed tart tin. Chill in the fridge for 8 hours or for 2 in the freezer. (I'm probably the most impatient person you'll ever meet so it's always the freezer for me!)

Scatter the cubed pumpkin on a roasting tray. Smear 2 tablespoons of the coconut oil over the pumpkin (it will be solid at room temperature, but soon melts in the oven). Sprinkle over the cinnamon and nutmeg and roast for 30–40 minutes. When cooked (they will be golden and soft), allow to cool for a few minutes then transfer to the food processor along with the dates, and blitz. (This will be a really thick mixture.) Add the almond milk, pumpkin pie spice, vanilla seeds and remaining 3 tablespoons of coconut oil, and blend until smooth. (Give it a taste — this mixture is all kinds of amazing!)

Spoon the filling over the pie base (use a spatula if you want to give it a fancy, swirly look) and place in the fridge for 6 hours (or freeze for 3). (I know it's a long time — that's why I told you to have a taste first!)

When set, drizzle with maple syrup and decorate with pecans and pumpkin seeds!

## SERVES 12

## TIPS

If you can't find any readymade pumpkin pie spice, it's easy to make your own (see page 58). And if you have any leftover pie crust, roll it into little balls and dip in coconut or chia seeds to make some extra raw treats.

## CRUST

80 g (½ cup) almonds, soaked and rinsed
60 g (½ cup) pecans, soaked and rinsed
80 g (½ cup) raisins
90 g (½ cup) medjool dates, pitted
3 tablespoons coconut oil, melted
3 tablespoons desiccated coconut
2 tablespoons maple syrup

## FILLING

360 g (3 cups) pumpkin, cut into 5 cm cubes
100 ml coconut oil
½ teaspoon ground cinnamon
¼ teaspoon ground nutmeg
180 g (1 cup) medjool dates, pitted
125 ml (½ cup) almond milk
1 teaspoon pumpkin pie spice
1 vanilla pod, split and scraped

## TOPPING

maple syrup
25 g (¼ cup) whole pecans
30 g (¼ cup) pumpkin seeds

# GOOEY STICKY DATE PUDDING

coconut oil, for greasing
360 g (2 cups) medjool
   dates, pitted and chopped
250 ml (1 cup) coconut oil
150 g (1½ cups) almond meal
1 teaspoon ground cinnamon
½ teaspoon gluten-free
   baking powder
pinch pink salt
5 eggs, lightly beaten
2 tablespoons apple cider
   vinegar
coconut ice cream,
   to serve, optional

**My dad loves sticky date pudding, and whenever we go out to dinner he just *has* to order it. For me, though, it's a sugar and wheat bomb, so here's my healthy version. (I just need to convince dad to switch to this creation…)**

Preheat the oven to 160°C. Grease a 23 cm cake tin with coconut oil.

Place the dates in a saucepan with 2 cups of water over a medium heat and bring to the boil. Simmer for 5 minutes, remove from the heat and add the coconut oil (which will melt). Allow to cool slightly then place in your food processor and blend until you have a smooth datey paste. Set aside.

Combine the almond meal, cinnamon, baking powder and salt in a large bowl. Fold through the egg and apple cider vinegar. Add half of the date paste and fold it through.

Pour all but ½ cup of the remaining date mixture into the base of the tin (the ½ cup is to use as a sauce at the end). Then on goes the almond meal cake mix. Bake for 30 minutes.

Remove from the oven and turn out onto a plate while it's still a little warm. Spoon over any sauce left in the cake tin. Serve warm with coconut ice cream (if using) and one last drizzle of your datey sauce. This is YUMBO!

SERVES 10

# BERRY CRUMBLE

**I love using berries in my foodie creations because they are little gems when it comes to health benefits. They're jam-packed with antioxidants, they make your skin glow and they're good for people with fructose malabsorption.**

Preheat the oven to 180°C.

Combine the berries, vanilla seeds, coconut sugar, lime juice and zest in a large bowl. Mix well with your hands (get those mitts in there!).

In another bowl combine the quinoa flakes, almond meal, shredded coconut and macadamias. Give them a stir then add the coconut oil and coconut sugar. Mix with your hands until nice and crumbly.

Place the berries in a baking dish (or divide between individual ramekins). Spread the crumble mixture over the berries and bake for 20–30 minutes or until the top is golden and the berries are oozing a little.

Serve with a scoop of coconut ice cream and a sprinkling of freshly torn mint leaves.

## SERVES 6

## TIPS

Feel free to replace any of the berries with ones you prefer (or can find). Frozen berries work just as well. This is also delicious with yoghurt.

300 g (2 cups) blueberries
150 g (1 cup) strawberries
130 g (1 cup) blackberries
125 g (1 cup) raspberries
1 vanilla pod, split and scraped
60 g (¼ cup) coconut sugar (double the quantity if you prefer it sweeter)
juice and zest of 1 lime
40 g (½ cup) quinoa flakes
3 tablespoons almond meal
3 tablespoons shredded coconut
80 g (½ cup) macadamia nuts, roughly chopped
125 ml (½ cup) coconut oil, melted
coconut ice cream, to serve
mint leaves, to garnish

# LEMON PIE BITES

150 g (1½ cups) almond meal

45 g (½ cup) desiccated
coconut

3 tablespoons maple syrup

juice of 3 lemons

zest of 1 lemon

1 vanilla pod, split and scraped

125 ml (½ cup) coconut oil,
melted

pinch pink salt

60 g (1 cup) shredded
coconut, for rolling

## TIPS

Rolling the bites is much easier
with slightly damp hands. Also,
desiccated coconut is fine
for rolling if you don't have
shredded. And use ½ teaspoon
pure vanilla powder if you're
out of vanilla pods.

**Lemon pie is another one of those delicious-sounding treats
that my body just can't handle, so I was determined to create
a healthy alternative. These bite-sized lemon balls are just
amazing, and *really* easy. Oh, and they freeze well, too.**

Pop all the ingredients (except the coconut for rolling) in your
food processor and blitz for 30 seconds. (You could do this
by hand, but the processor makes these little gems taste like
heavenly lemon mousse.)

Place a teaspoonful of the mixture into your palm and shape
into a little ball. Roll in the shredded coconut and place on a
plate. Repeat until you've used up all of the mixture (this is a
fun one to do with children). Refrigerate for about 20 minutes
or until firm. Store in a plastic container in the fridge or freezer
and you've got the perfect treat for any time of day!

MAKES 24

- **Pan Mac:** For making this magic happen. Dreams really do come true. Thank you.
- **Mary Small:** You're one of the most inspiring and creative humans I know, and you just make things happen. Thank you for your vision and guidance.
- **Ellie Smith:** Your quirk and passion are so contagious to work with, I feel real blessed we got to work on the creative jazz together.
- **Clare Marshall:** Thank you for being such a gem and a chilled soul to work with.
- **Oscar Gordon:** O, you are amazing, your guidance and knowledge are things I will always respect and be so grateful for.
- **Armelle Habib:** Photographer of the book, you were such a dream to work with. Thank you.
- **Deb Kaloper:** One talented food stylist, your creations are magic.
- **Paige Anderson:** Your creative eye is genius, the food styling and flowers made this shoot bliss.
- **Emma Christian:** Talented food guru, thank you for all your work on this shoot.
- **Beckie Littler:** More helping hands on the shoot, you were so great to work with.
- **John Laurie:** You are a genius who makes magic happen. Thank you.
- **Linda Raymond:** You believe in me no matter what, and you're brave enough to pull me into line when I need it. Thank you.
- **Mum, Dad and Tristan:** For putting up with my crazy lifestyle and fitting in hangouts with bizarre schedules.
- **Karina Duncan:** You're an awesome friend who I feel so lucky to have in my life. You've been a huge part of this journey. Thank you.
- **Melanie Tjoeng:** Epic soul and just as epic a photographer.
- **All of my yoga teachers:** Practising yoga has kept me calm and zen during this whole process which can normally be so stressful. And yoga brings me bliss — thank you for giving me that gift.
- **Faustina Agolley:** You are the mate who loves me for who I am and yet inspires me to be more. Thank you.
- **Lucy Roach:** For being the first person to give me a chance on live telly. Without you, none of these books would have existed.
- **Jad Patrick:** Real mates are hard to come by and you are definitely one of them. Thank you, hobbit Jaddles.
- **Maddie Daisy Dixon:** The ultimate biophila buddy! Here's to being nature nerds.
- **Kane Dignum:** For your wisdom and belief in me. Here's to spreading our wings and living the dream.
- **Recipe testers:** You are all so unreal, thank you so much! The recipes would have been a bit higgledy-piggledy if it wasn't for you. Tash, Bridget, Mietta, Lucy, Jess, Belle, Faustina, Amie, Calypso, Kat and my number one tester, Dad.
- **Amber Clayton:** Pumpy Jackson, such a cosmic soul, so rapt we've crossed paths.
- **Glen Mackay:** One awesome cameraman, who laughs at all my jokes, even if they're not funny.
- **Belle Gibson:** For being an inspiring food buddy.
- **Dexter Gordon:** You've been an integral part of this family from the very beginning. Thank you so much for your hard work and all the laughs!
- **Bronwyn Hofert:** This lady makes things happen, another inspiring soul.
- **Glenn Tebble:** For your amazing plates and bowls — your creations are truly amazing and I feel very lucky I get to work with them.
- **Gorman:** For decking me out in awesome clothes. Thank you.
- **Stevie:** Time and time again for decking me out in unreal clothes. Thank you.
- **Caitlin and Lisa from One Management:** For your help and support.
- **Miriam Cannell:** You worked your magic on the last book and you've done it again. Thank you so much, M – love working with you!
- **Allison Colpoys:** Thank you for your creative, magical brain. You've brought this book to life.
- **Hannah Marshall:** Epic make-up artist who made me feel like a natural beauty.

INDEX

**A PLUM BOOK**

First published in 2014 by
Pan Macmillan Australia Pty Limited
Level 25, 1 Market Street,
Sydney, NSW 2000, Australia

Level 1, 15–19 Claremont Street,
South Yarra, Victoria 3141, Australia

Design by Allison Colpoys
Edited by Miriam Cannell
Index by Jo Rudd
Photography by Armelle Habib
Prop styling by Paige Anderson
Food styling by Deborah Kaloper
Food preparation by Deborah Kaloper and Emma Christian
Typeset by Pauline Haas
Colour reproduction by Splitting Image Colour Studio
Printed and bound in China

A CIP catalogue record for this book is available from
the National Library of Australia.

The publisher would like to thank the following for their generosity
in providing props for the book: the Junk Company, Tara Shackell
Ceramics, Anchor Ceramics, the Mod Collective, Bonnie and Neil,
Hut 13 and Shelley Panton Pottery.

10 9 8 7 6 5 4